STRENGTHEN
One Another
IN THE LORD

STRENGTHEN
One Another
IN THE LORD

TALKS FROM THE 2018
BYU WOMEN'S CONFERENCE

DESERET
BOOK

SALT LAKE CITY, UTAH

She Will Find What Is Lost, page 145, © 2012 Brian Kershisnik. Used by permission.

Library of Congress Cataloging-in-Publication Data

Names: Women's Conference (2018 : Brigham Young University), author.
Title: Strengthen one another in the Lord : talks from the 2018 BYU Women's Conference.
Description: Salt Lake City, Utah : Deseret Book, [2019] | Includes bibliographical references.
Identifiers: LCCN 2018047212 | ISBN 9781629725666 (hardbound : alk. paper)
Subjects: LCSH: The Church of Jesus Christ of Latter-day Saints—Doctrines. | Mormon Church—Doctrines. | Mormon women—Conduct of life—Congresses. | Mormon women—Religious life—Congresses. | LCGFT: Conference papers and proceedings.
Classification: LCC BX8656 .W6 2018 | DDC 248.8/43088289332—dc23
LC record available at https://lccn.loc.gov/2018047212

Printed in the United States of America
Publishers Printing, Salt Lake City, UT

10   9   8   7   6   5   4   3   2   1

Contents

THE WATCHMAN ON THE TOWER

LISTEN TO A PROPHET'S VOICE

Kathy S. Andersen

WITH REMARKS BY ELDER NEIL L. ANDERSEN

On March 31, 2018, we each had the privilege of raising an arm to sustain President Russell M. Nelson as a prophet, seer, revelator, and President of The Church of Jesus Christ of Latter-day Saints. The feelings of those two "never to be forgotten" days will remain in our hearts forever. It was a remarkable experience punctuated with heavenly power and deep feelings that Jesus is the Christ, the Son of God, the "chief corner stone" of His Church with a foundation of apostles and prophets (see Ephesians 2:19–20).

Elder Neil L. Andersen of the Quorum of the Twelve (my husband, I love him so much), explained one of the reasons that the Lord has given us a prophet:

"Why do we follow the prophet? Because the Lord Jesus Christ has called him and designated him as His watchman on the tower.

"Carcassonne is a remarkable walled city in France that has stood since medieval times. Tall towers surge upward from its protected walls, built for watchmen who stood on those towers day and night, keeping their attention riveted in the distance for the enemy. When the watchman saw an enemy approaching, his warning voice protected the people of Carcassonne from the impending danger they could not see.

"A prophet is a watchman on the tower, protecting us from spiritual dangers we may not see.

"The Lord said to Ezekiel, 'I have set thee a watchman unto the house of Israel; therefore thou shalt hear the word [from] my mouth, and warn them from me' (Ezekiel 33:7).

"We often speak of our need to follow the prophet, but consider this heavy burden the Lord places upon His prophet: 'If thou dost not speak to warn the wicked . . . , [and] that wicked man . . . die in his iniquity; . . . his blood will I require at thine hand' (Ezekiel 33:8)."[1]

I have stood on those walls of Carcassonne with my husband and children and climbed into the towers where the watchmen stood imagining the people in the city below who could not see the danger.

We are like the people in Carcassonne. "[The] prophet is [our] watchman on the tower."[2]

One of my favorite stories in the Old Testament is found in 2 Kings 5. You will remember that Namaan had leprosy and went to the prophet Elisha to be healed. The prophet instructed that Namaan should simply wash in the River Jordan seven times to be healed. Naaman protested, but finally he did wash in the River Jordan seven times, and he was healed.

How did Namaan learn of the Prophet Elisha? The Syrians had brought a little maid captive out of Israel. "She waited on Naaman's wife" (2 Kings 5:2). The little maid was the one who was so brave and filled with such faith that she declared to those who did not know of the prophet, "Would God my lord

[Namaan] were with the prophet that is in Samaria! for [the prophet, Elisha] would [heal] him of his leprosy" (2 Kings 5:3).

Remarkably, they believed her—a "little maid." It seems almost impossible, but it is true. Her faith, her testimony, her conviction, and her absolute belief in Elisha, the prophet of God, led Namaan to the tent door of Elisha and to a miraculous experience. How did one so young have such an absolute faith in the prophet of God?

I was in Africa with my husband several years ago. We visited a family in their home. There was a paper picture of the Savior and a paper picture of the prophet fastened to their wall. As my husband was talking to the children, the mother quietly came and stood by me. She looked at me and said, "Please ask your husband to tell the prophet that we pray for him—that he will receive revelation from God—so that we can teach our children what they need to do." Beautifully simple, spiritually profound.

This is the faith of members of the Church all over the world.

In the Sunday morning session of the April 2018 general conference, President Russell M. Nelson gave us a glimpse of the glorious days he sees ahead. He said, "Our Savior and Redeemer, Jesus Christ, will perform some of His mightiest works between now and when He comes again. We will see miraculous indications that God the Father and His Son, Jesus Christ, preside over this Church in majesty and glory."[3]

Isn't it breathtaking to think about the marvelous events in front of us?

That Sunday morning, President Nelson, acting as God's watchman on the tower, also gave us a glimpse of something else—grave spiritual danger ahead. He warned: "In coming days, it will not be possible to survive spiritually without the guiding, directing, comforting, and constant influence of the Holy Ghost."[4]

If we believe that is a warning from God—and we surely do—then we realize that we are in harm's way, and so are those we love, which makes it imperative for us to move to safety. That Sunday morning in general conference, President Nelson gave us very specific direction on what to do:

"Choose to do the spiritual work required to enjoy the gift of the Holy Ghost and hear the voice of the Spirit more frequently and more clearly."[5]

"I urge you," President Nelson said, "to stretch beyond your current spiritual ability to receive personal revelation."[6]

"My beloved brothers and sisters, I plead with you to increase your spiritual capacity to receive revelation. Let this Easter Sunday be a defining moment in your life."[7]

President Nelson's prophetic warning was as serious as any I have ever heard in my lifetime. That is a role of a prophet, a seer, a revelator. He doesn't predict, he prophesies, meaning this will happen "in the coming days."

Should we be concerned? Yes! Do we need to be afraid? No! Because there is a path to safety. Let's read one brief excerpt from the prophet's Sunday morning message giving specific direction on how we can "survive spiritually":

"Brothers and sisters, how can we become the men and women—the Christlike servants—the Lord needs us to be? How can we find answers to questions that perplex us? If Joseph Smith's transcendent experience in the Sacred Grove teaches us anything, it is that the heavens are open and that God speaks to His children.

"The Prophet Joseph Smith set a pattern for us to follow in

resolving our questions. Drawn to the promise of James that if we lack wisdom we may ask of God (see James 1:5), the boy Joseph took his question directly to Heavenly Father. He sought personal revelation, and his seeking opened this last dispensation.

"In like manner, what will your seeking open for you? What wisdom do you lack? What do you feel an urgent need to know or understand? Follow the example of the Prophet Joseph. Find a quiet place where you can regularly go. Humble yourself before God. Pour out your heart to your Heavenly Father. Turn to Him for answers and for comfort.

"Pray in the name of Jesus Christ about your concerns, your fears, your weaknesses—yes, the very longings of your heart. And then listen! Write the thoughts that come to your mind. Record your feelings and follow through with actions that you are prompted to take. As you repeat this process day after day, month after month, year after year, you will 'grow into the principle of revelation.'

"Does God really *want* to speak to you? Yes!"[8]

President Nelson is teaching us how we can be safe. How important is it for us to study his words and follow his counsel? Our spiritual survival depends upon it.

Think about what you remember right now from that excerpt. What did the prophet specifically counsel us to do? Have we thought about it? Have we tried to do what he asked us to do?

For example, President Nelson asked these questions:

- "What will your seeking open for you?"
- "What wisdom do you lack?"
- "What do you feel an urgent need to know or understand?"[9]

Then the prophet gave us very specific counsel:

- "Follow the example of the Prophet Joseph."
- "Find a quiet place where you can regularly go."[10]

Let me just interject a thought here. Beyond just listening to the watchman on the tower, the people in Carcassonne who wanted to survive had to move to safety. They couldn't just keep doing what they were doing. When the prophet warns, we have to respond if we want to be safe.

Remember Namaan? The prophet Elisha asked him to wash in the River Jordan seven times. Another river would not work, and washing three times would not work.

President Nelson asked us to "find a quiet place where [we] can regularly go" to pray. Let's use this as an example of something very specific. We might think, "There is no place in my house that is quiet." That may be true. But if we really want to follow the prophet, we can find a place—God will help us find some place that is quiet where we "can regularly go" because that simple thing is what the prophet asked us to do.

President Nelson continued:

- "Humble yourself before God."
- "Pour out your heart to your Heavenly Father."
- "Turn to Him for answers and for comfort."
- "Pray in the name of Jesus Christ about your concerns, your fears, your weaknesses—yes, the very longings of your heart."[11]

Then President Nelson gave us this specific direction:

- "And then listen!"
- "Write the thoughts that come to your mind."

- "Record your feelings and follow through with actions that you are prompted to take."[12]

Like you, I have prayed since I was a child but I haven't always prayed like President Nelson suggested in this general conference until the last few weeks. I will tell you that I have felt something different, like "the dews from heaven distilling" upon my soul.[13]

Look at President Nelson's promise to us: "As you repeat this process day after day, month after month, year after year, you will 'grow into the principle of revelation.'"[14]

We will have that blessing in our lives as we follow the counsel of the prophet. That is God's promise to us. He said, "Whether by mine own voice or by the voice of my servants, it is the same" (Doctrine and Covenants 1:38).

This is only one example from a two-minute excerpt. President Nelson warned us, counseled us, and promised us extraordinary blessings for doing some relatively simple things throughout his forty-three minutes of messages those two days. Is it worth the time and effort to study his words and do what the Lord has asked? We answer with a resounding, "Yes," because it is worth everything to us and those we love.

In the April 2018 general conference, President Dallin H. Oaks spoke about "how the Israelites were plagued by fiery serpents. Many people died. . . . When Moses prayed for relief, he was inspired to make 'a serpent of brass, and put it upon a pole.'" Then, if a person was bitten by one of the fiery serpents, and looked up at the serpent of brass on the pole, he did not die, but he lived. "Such a small thing," President Oaks said, "for such a miraculous result!"[15]

Try it. Just look up. For most people, that is very simple, very easy. So we ask ourselves, "Why didn't they just look up?"

It was Nephi who taught us that "because of the simpleness of the way, or the easiness of it, there were many [of the Israelites] who perished" (1 Nephi 17:41).

A painting by Judith Mehr titled *Moses and the Brass Serpent* fascinates me.[16]

There are a few people in the painting that are looking up. But many turned their backs and walked away. Why didn't they just look up and live? It was such an easy thing to do.

After the past conference, I put little paper copies of this picture in a few places in our home as a reminder to me that nothing that President Nelson asked us to do was impossible or even extraordinarily difficult.

We can do all that we have been asked to do. If we really want to follow the prophet with exactness, God will help us do it.

Think about these comments from past Presidents of the Church about the great importance of the messages from general conference:

President Harold B. Lee suggested that the conference talks "be the guide to [our] walk and talk during the next six months. These are the important matters," he said, "the Lord sees fit to reveal to this people in this day."[17]

President Spencer W. Kimball said of the conference talks: "No text or volume outside the standard works of the Church should have such a prominent place on your personal library shelves."[18]

President Ezra Taft Benson said, "For the next six months, your conference edition of the *Ensign* should stand next to your standard works and be referred to frequently."[19]

One of the lessons we can learn from these statements is that in the messages of general conference, we are receiving direction from

God about where to place our focus for the next six months. For me, that is enormously helpful. Very simple. Very clear. Here is the focus for the next six months from the Lord through His servants.

President Gordon B. Hinckley and President Thomas S. Monson gave us similar counsel.

And our beloved prophet, President Russell M. Nelson, counseled us: "I exhort you to study the messages of this conference frequently—even repeatedly—during the next six months. Conscientiously look for ways to incorporate these messages in your family home evenings, your gospel teaching, your conversations with family and friends, and even your discussions with those not of our faith."[20]

Look at the significant blessings he promised us for doing this: "Many good people will respond to the truths taught in this conference when offered in love." Can you imagine what that might mean for missionaries and all of us who would like to share the gospel? "And your desire to obey will be enhanced as you remember and reflect upon what you have felt these past two days."[21]

That is a remarkable promise—"[our] desire to obey will be enhanced."

President Nelson did not ask us to wash in the River Jordan seven times—that was Elisha's counsel for Namaan in his day. President Nelson did not ask us to look up at the brass serpent on a pole. That was Moses's counsel for the Israelites in their day.

This is our day. This is our time. We have to know what we have been asked to do by the prophet of our day, President Russell M. Nelson, and then we have to have the faith and courage to simply do it. "We thank thee, O God, for a prophet / To guide us"[22] home—home to a waiting Father who gave us life, and home to His loving Son, whose sacrifice offers us eternal life.

With raised hands we sustained the First Presidency and Quorum of the Twelve as prophets, seers, and revelators. They are watchmen on the tower. Their ordination carries such an immense responsibility for them, but brings such enormous safety to us.

I am so honored that my husband, Elder Neil L. Andersen of the Quorum of the Twelve, is with us today. May his concluding testimony bring a most sacred and confirming witness to our souls.

• • •

Elder Andersen: I love Kathy Andersen very, very much. She's a person of profound faith and enormous spiritual depth. And although I'm very happy to always bear my testimony, it is the love I have for her that makes me willing to participate this morning.

President Boyd K. Packer coined a phrase that I think might be helpful today. He would say, "What will you remember when you've forgotten everything?" When you come to a conference like this one, with so many inspiring speakers, you have to ask yourself, "What will I remember long after my notes have been misplaced and my mind is on other things?"

In reflecting on Kathy's beautiful message, I would hope that you would remember what our family has learned from her for more than forty years. She, from my very first days of knowing her, would take the talks of the prophets and apostles, especially of the President of the Church, and would study every sentence, carefully noting the promises, the blessings, and the specific counsel that was given. And, perhaps more important than her study, she would attentively incorporate the teachings into our family life. Thanks to her, for the past forty years, we have experienced the life-changing inspiration of the Lord as it has come through His ordained prophets.

I've watched President Russell M. Nelson through my time as a member of the Quorum of the Twelve Apostles, as he has prayed over every word, pondered every sentence, and thought deeply about every principle he would share in general conference. I think the principle to try to remember from Kathy's powerful address would be: Let's look closer at what the Prophet is saying, prayerfully asking what the Lord is instructing us through His chosen servant. The first question is if the hand of the Lord is upon President Nelson, and if what President Nelson is teaching is the Lord's counsel for us today. The second very important question is if we have the courage to adjust our lives to follow his counsel.

I give you my witness that over and over again, we can receive that confirming spiritual impression that President Nelson's words are the Lord's teachings specifically for us. Just yesterday, as President Nelson walked into the temple with his two counselors, shook my hand and looked me in the eyes, once again, just as when I stood and sustained him on March 31, 2018, or as we in the Quorum of the Twelve had our hands upon his head on January 14, 2018, I felt the Lord's power upon him. The Lord accomplishes His purposes in many ways, but a principal way is through His Church, complete with His Priesthood, The Church of Jesus Christ of Latter-day Saints—this small band of believers across all nations, all cultures, all languages, all races. As Israel is gathered and as preparations are made for the Savior's return, I give you my sure and certain witness that Jesus is the Christ, the Son of God, that He lives, that He is resurrected, and that He guides His holy work upon the earth.

A New and Holier Way of Ministering

Strengthen One Another in the Lord

Kevin J Worthen

Let me testify that revelation is alive and active in God's Church today. We have seen it in abundance in the most recent general conference (April 2018)—from the solemn assembly, where a new prophet and president of the Church was sustained, to the announcement of a new, unified effort to fulfill the Lord's commandment that we love one another. I join Elder Jeffrey R. Holland in bearing witness that this recent "rush of revelation" is but one example "of the revelation that has guided this Church from its beginning."[1]

Let me bear witness in a more specific way that that same kind of divine revelation and guidance has simultaneously been operating in other aspects of God's work in ways that may not have been as evident. Knowing that this new emphasis on Christlike ministering was to be announced at the April 2018 general conference, God has, in the preceding months, been preparing the way for that work to be accelerated, even when those who were being inspired may not have recognized the full purposes for which they were being prompted. President Henry B. Eyring noted this phenomenon in his priesthood session address when he said that "time after time in recent weeks, members of the Church have acted in my presence as if somehow they had anticipated what the Lord was going to do."[2]

Viewed in retrospect—as such events are usually most clearly viewed—I can see how this has happened with respect to this women's conference. The theme for this women's conference is "Strengthen One Another in the Lord." That theme is amazingly consistent with the new emphasis on ministering. In fact, one might describe ministering as an effort to strengthen one another in the Lord. The theme is so well adapted to highlight, explore, and explicate the new emphasis on ministering that was announced just weeks ago that future observers who are not careful will erroneously assume that those responsible selected the women's conference theme *after* the new emphasis on ministering was announced, or at least with full knowledge that the announcement was coming. But I know from personal experience that the women's conference theme was selected in the early fall of 2017, many months before any public announcements about any changes to quorums or visiting teaching were made. And I am confident that those involved in the selection of that theme were not privy to any special inside information or involved in some intricate effort to coordinate the timing of events and announcements—at least not any effort orchestrated by mortal beings. The fact that the women's conference theme so well complements the call for ministering that sounded so clearly in general conference can be attributed only to what some have called celestial correlation.

Indeed, viewing events in the last fifteen years in light of the recent announcements reveals how the Lord has efficiently and effectively—though not always obviously—been preparing us, as a people, to be able to strengthen one another in the Lord in the new and holier way of ministering that was outlined in general conference.

At the risk of oversimplifying and maybe even underestimating the full significance of some key changes that have been effectuated in the Church in the last fifteen years, and guided only by my own not-fully-adequate, post-hoc observation, let me outline, at a general level, one of the ways changes in the last fifteen years have prepared us, as a people, to embrace and carry out this new and holier ministering effort.

A COMMON THREAD

I begin with the release and implementation of the manual *Preach My Gospel: A Guide to Missionary Service* in 2004, which changed the way full-time missionaries operated throughout the world. Among the more notable changes was a shift from memorized, pre-scripted lessons to more flexible, Spirit-driven teaching in which missionaries would "'master the concepts of the lessons [but] . . . teach the concepts in their own words under the guiding influence of the Holy Spirit.'"[3] Because this new form of teaching depended on the Spirit rather than on a prewritten uniform text, the *Preach My Gospel* manual contained "chapters that [gave] extremely valuable information on how to recognize and understand the guidance of the Holy Spirit."[4]

The most obvious benefit of this new approach was a more effective and powerful presentation of gospel truths to those whom the missionaries taught. But there can be little doubt that an equally important result of the *Preach My Gospel* manual was a cohort of returned missionaries who were better able to recognize and respond to the guidance of the Holy Ghost in both their daily lives and their future church service.

This emphasis on Spirit-driven gospel teaching was expanded

beyond the missionary effort in 2013 with the adoption of the *Come, Follow Me* curriculum for youth.[5] Once again there was a shift from pre-scripted lessons to more flexible, individualized teaching in which the key component was the ability to receive, recognize, and follow the promptings of the Holy Ghost. For those youth leaders who had learned and applied the principles of *Preach My Gospel* as missionaries, this was an easy transition, as it was merely the application of that program to a different setting. This was old hat to them. Not so for some of the rest of us. As I watched some of us older members—who had not had the benefit of a *Preach My Gospel* mission experience—struggle a bit with this transition from reliance on a scripted lesson plan to a more Spirit-driven teaching method, I wondered if the Lord had waited to fully reveal the *Come, Follow Me* youth curriculum until there was a critical mass of returned missionary youth leaders steeped in the principles of *Preach My Gospel* to carry forth the program with full energy.

The next step came with the announcement in August 2017 that the *Come, Follow Me* curriculum would now be rolled out to the adults in their priesthood and Relief Society lessons.[6] Again, this was a shift from using pre-scripted lessons to a more flexible, individualized form of teaching that depends on the guidance of the Holy Ghost, in both the preparation and presentation of the lessons.

That then brings us to the April 2018 general conference. Only months after the *Come, Follow Me* curriculum was fully implemented among both the youth and the adults, we received a new vision of ministering. While the ministering effort may seem unconnected to the teaching and curriculum changes in *Preach My Gospel* and *Come, Follow Me*, in retrospect I see a common thread throughout all these changes: a shift (now seismic) from a pre-scripted, formulaic teaching method to a Spirit-directed, flexible, individualized effort to bring people unto Christ. By learning to teach in the Savior's way, we are now better prepared to minister in the Savior's way.

A NEW VISION OF MINISTERING

The new vision of ministering is, therefore, merely a continuation of the trend that I first noted with *Preach My Gospel.* Like these prior curriculum changes, this new vision of ministering—this new and holier way of strengthening one another in the Lord—requires us to set aside the pre-scripted lesson previously found in the *Ensign* and become more capable of recognizing and responding to the Spirit.

Given that trend, it should not be surprising that in his Sunday morning general conference address, President Russell M. Nelson emphasized the need for us to refine and enhance our ability to receive revelation. Consider these key observations and invitations from that talk:

"One of the things the Spirit has repeatedly impressed upon my mind since my new calling as President of the Church is how willing the Lord is to reveal His mind and will. The privilege of receiving revelation is one of the greatest gifts of God to His children. . . .

"If we are to have any hope of sifting through the myriad of voices and the philosophies of men that attack truth, we must learn to receive revelation.

"Our Savior and Redeemer, Jesus Christ, will perform some of His mightiest works between now and when He comes again. We will see miraculous indications that God the Father and His Son, Jesus Christ, preside over this Church in majesty and glory. But in coming days, it will not be possible to survive spiritually without the guiding, directing, comforting, and constant influence of the Holy Ghost.

"My beloved brothers and sisters, I plead with you to increase your spiritual capacity to receive revelation. Let this Easter Sunday be a defining moment in your life. Choose to do the spiritual work required to enjoy the gift of the Holy Ghost and hear the voice of the Spirit more frequently and more clearly."[7]

Given the pattern that I have seen, I believe that President Nelson's heartfelt plea that we increase our spiritual capacity to receive revelation was not provided just so we can more fully carry out this new vision of ministering but also to prepare us for even greater challenges and opportunities that lie ahead. I am confident that the rush of revelation we have witnessed in the past month is not the culmination of the pattern I have noticed but merely the latest edition. Indeed, I believe that we are witnessing an acceleration in that pattern. In that regard, I note that it was eight years after *Preach My Gospel* that the *Come, Follow Me* curriculum was implemented for the youth. It was only four years between that and the full implementation of that curriculum for the adults and only a few months after the announcement of that new curriculum when the new vision of ministering was announced. The changes seem to be coming faster and faster, which is further evidence that the Lord is hastening His "work in its time" (Doctrine and Covenants 88:73). Stay tuned and buckle up. I am confident that there is more to come.

INSPIRED MINISTERING

But rather than speculating about the future, or dwelling too much on the past, we should consider how we can more fully embrace and implement the new vision we have been given. With that goal in mind, let me suggest five things we might do to enhance our ability to strengthen one another in the Lord through inspired ministering.

1. Understand the Full Purpose and Ultimate Aim of Ministering

The first suggestion is illustrated by a traditional story of which there are many versions:

There was once a Swiss guard who worked at the border of Austria. He worked there for many years and took a great deal of pride in his work.

One morning an Austrian man arrived at the border, riding a bicycle. On the front of his bike was a basket filled with sand. Another guard might simply have waved him through, but the Swiss guard did not. Instead, he brought out a special comb he kept for just such a purpose and began to sift through the sand in the basket. You see, he suspected the Austrian might be a smuggler. Finding nothing but sand, however, he waved the man through.

The same thing happened the next day, and the day after that. Though he never found anything, he kept on looking, day after day, for thirty years. Finally, one day the Swiss guard spoke to the Austrian man. "I must ask you a question," he said, "that has been on my mind for many years. This is my last day of work. Today I shall retire. And all these years, I suspect you have been a smuggler. Now I ask you, for I must know—are you indeed a smuggler?"

The Austrian man hesitated, and the Swiss guard reassured him, "Do not worry. I give you my word of honour that I will not prosecute you. But I must know."

"Very well," said the Austrian. "Then I will tell you. I am indeed a smuggler."

"Ah-ha!" said the guard. "I knew it! But each day I look

through your basket and find nothing but sand. Tell me, please, what have you been smuggling?"

"Bicycles."[8]

I worry just a bit that we will become so caught up in the excitement of this new emphasis on ministering and so focused on the details of what it requires in implementation that we, like the Swiss border guard, will lose sight of the bigger picture. For example, we might spend time deliberating about what counts as a ministering visit or as a ministering interview. In my view, such discussion is time fruitlessly spent combing through the sand in the basket. To the extent we find that happening, we should reevaluate what we are doing, lest we miss the truly important things God wants to accomplish with this new effort. We will be more constant, more efficient, and more effective in our efforts if we understand the full purpose, the ultimate aim, of our ministering efforts.

The Lord has asked us to engage in this new and holier ministering effort not just to relieve the temporal, emotional, and spiritual suffering of our fellow brothers and sisters—as important as that is to do. Feeding the poor, clothing the naked, and relieving the burdens of God's children is extremely important and essential work. We should do all we can in that regard, and, in doing so, we should partner with others who have that same end in mind. However, God, in His wisdom and love, wants to accomplish much more than that with our ministering efforts. He wants us to do something that we in the true Church of Jesus Christ are uniquely positioned to do. Our Heavenly Father's goal is—and our goal should therefore also be—the exaltation of all of His children. That requires that we not only comfort and lift the afflicted but that we help them draw closer to Christ through making and keeping sacred, exalting covenants. As President Nelson put it:

"Our message to the world is simple and sincere: we invite all of God's children on both sides of the veil to come unto their Savior, receive the blessings of the holy temple, have enduring joy, and qualify for eternal life."[9]

That is our goal. Strengthening one another in the Lord through ministering is merely a means to that end. If we fail to understand that, we run the risk that we will be diverted off our main course, and we will soon focus on the sand in the basket and not on the bicycle. This will not only cause us to lose enthusiasm and energy as we get bogged down in details, but can also cause us to fail to recognize and take advantage of all the tools we have been given to aid us, both in the implementation of the new vision of ministering and, more important, in the larger work of exalting all of God's children.

Let me give one example. Three years ago our leaders asked us to make efforts to enhance our Sabbath-day worship at church and at home. With all the energy and excitement that surrounds this new vision of ministering, some may think that it is time to lay aside efforts to enhance Sabbath-day worship so that we can concentrate on ministering, viewing the former as a substitute for the latter. If we do that, we will miss the common overarching goal of both efforts, and our ability to accomplish either will be greatly diminished.

As we have consistently been reminded—but I fear we do not always recall—the purpose of the effort to enhance our Sabbath-day worship was not merely to increase sacrament meeting attendance but to increase our faith in Heavenly Father and His Son, Jesus Christ. The increase in our faith in God that comes from enhanced Sabbath-day worship will enhance our ability to minister and to strengthen one another in several ways.

For example, as previously noted, ministering in a new and holier way requires that we be more open and responsive to the promptings of the Holy Ghost. Sabbath-day worship facilitates that kind of spiritual development. Proper Sabbath-day worship allows us to renew our baptismal covenant so that we may become clean again. Such purity opens the channels of revelation, as President Nelson taught us.[10] Enhanced Sabbath-day worship also helps us create in our homes an atmosphere in which the Holy Ghost can abide, thereby expanding the scope of holy places in which we can receive inspiration that is essential to ministering.

Similarly, enhanced Sabbath-day worship increases our love for our Heavenly Father and His Son. As we increase our faith in God through Sabbath-day worship, our love for God will increase. The more we know and trust God, the more we will love Him. That, in turn, causes us to want to worship Him more fully. Thus, as President Nelson noted in 2015, "Faith in God engenders a love for the Sabbath; faith in the Sabbath engenders a love for God."[11]

Love of God is at the heart of the new ministering effort. The 2018 letter from the First Presidency announcing the new adjustments begins with reference to the two great commandments:

"Thou shalt love the Lord thy God with all thy heart, and with all thy soul, and with all thy mind. . . .

" . . . Thou shalt love thy neighbour as thyself" (Matthew 22:37, 39).[12]

As the words between these two commandments make clear, the order of the commandments is important. The first, to love God, is the "great commandment"; "the second is like unto it" (Matthew 22:38–39). If we want to fully love our fellow beings, we need to first love God with all our heart, soul, and mind. As we do so, we will more fully feel God's love for us, and we will more completely understand what true love is. An increase in our love for God will, in turn, increase our love for His children, our fellow beings. And as we love our fellow beings more, we will more naturally want to minister to them, to strengthen them in the Lord. The increased love for God that proper Sabbath-day worship engenders therefore increases our ability to minister to others, and both efforts advance God's work to exalt His children.

Thus, enhanced Sabbath-day worship not only better prepares us to receive the revelation necessary to minister in a new and holier way but also helps provide the motivation we need to engage in that critical work.

If we keep our focus on the ultimate goal of our ministering efforts—rather than on the less important details—we will find that other divinely inspired teachings and programs are part of the same sacred work and that all aspects of the work can combine in new and powerful ways to accomplish that ultimate goal.

In that regard, we are witnessing the fulfillment of Paul's remarkable prophecy "that in the dispensation of the fulness of times [God] might gather together *in one all things* in Christ, both which are in heaven, and which are on earth" (Ephesians 1:10; emphasis added). All the changes I have discussed—from the introduction of *Preach My Gospel* to enhanced Sabbath-day worship to ministering in a new and holier way—are being brought together in one great effort to advance the work of salvation on both sides of the veil.

If we are to fully succeed in our ministering efforts, we must keep in mind the larger purpose and look for ways in which other seemingly disconnected efforts can be brought together in one to accomplish that larger purpose.

2. Develop Key Characteristics: Charity and the Companionship of the Holy Ghost

A second way we can enhance our ability to implement this new vision of ministering is to develop two key characteristics that are at the heart of the ministering effort—indeed, at the heart of all our efforts to advance God's work. President Henry B. Eyring noted these two critical elements in two different talks in the April 2018 general conference. At the Saturday priesthood session, he stated:

"Municipal wards, companies, and strengthened quorums have all required at least *two things* to be successful in the Lord's intent to have His Saints care for each other in the way He cares for them. They succeed when the Saints feel the love of Christ for each other above their self-interest. The scriptures call it 'charity . . . the pure love of Christ' (Moroni 7:47). And they succeed when the Holy Ghost guides the caregiver to know what the Lord knows is best for the person whom He is trying to help."[13]

To make sure we did not miss the point, President Eyring made it again in his Sunday morning general conference address:

"It seems there are two things [all great ministers] do. Great ministers have qualified for the Holy Ghost as a nearly constant companion. And they have qualified for the gift of charity, which is the pure love of Christ."[14]

Charity and the companionship of the Holy Ghost are critical to the success of our efforts to minister in a new and holier way. These two gifts from God mutually reinforce one another in the ministering effort. The Holy Ghost can sanctify us, which enables us to more fully feel God's love for His children. And the expression of love for others facilitates receipt of the Holy Ghost. As President Eyring explained:

"It seems to me that we receive the Holy Spirit best when we are focused on serving others. . . . The Holy Ghost can . . . help us in our lifelong quest to have the gift of charity bestowed upon us."[15]

Both of these characteristics are gifts from God, and each is a gift that the Book of Mormon indicates comes in large part as a result of earnest, constant prayer. Mormon concluded his instruction on charity with a fervent plea:

"Wherefore, my beloved brethren, pray unto the Father with all the energy of heart, that ye may be filled with this love, which he hath bestowed upon all who are true followers of his Son, Jesus Christ" (Moroni 7:48).

Those on the American continent who were eyewitnesses of the resurrected Christ had a similar experience with the gift of the Holy Ghost. As these Saints waited for the return of Christ on the second day of His visit, they gathered together to pray:

"And they did pray for that which they most desired; and they desired that the Holy Ghost should be given unto them" (3 Nephi 19:9).

Thus charity and the Holy Ghost are essential to the work of ministering. They mutually reinforce each other in that process, and, not surprisingly, both come as a gift from God, granted in part in response to earnest prayer. If we can develop our capacity to receive and act upon these two key gifts, our ministering efforts will be greatly magnified.

3. Recognize and Learn from Examples of Ministering

The third suggestion for enhancing our ability to strengthen one another through ministering is to recognize more fully all the ways and all the contexts in which ministering occurs and to better understand the great impact that such efforts can have.

Because we are no longer tethered to the pre-scripted monthly message and format that characterized home and visiting teaching, some may feel uncertain and hesitant about what ministering looks like and what they should do. Recognizing that ultimately the answers will come through individualized inspiration prompted by our love for those to whom we minister, it is still sometimes helpful to have some examples in mind to jump-start the revelatory process. Fortunately there are plenty of sources for such examples.

We can begin with the inspired insights provided by our leaders at the recent general conference. For example, Sister Jean B. Bingham powerfully noted:

"Sometimes we think we have to do something grand and heroic to 'count' as serving our neighbors. Yet simple acts of service can have profound effects on others—as well as on ourselves. . . .

"Ministering can be done in a great variety of individualized ways. So what does it look like?

"Ministering looks like . . . going for a walk, getting together for a game night, offering service, or even serving together. It looks like visiting in person or talking on the phone or chatting online or texting. It looks like delivering a birthday card and cheering at a soccer game. It looks like sharing a scripture or quote from a conference talk that would be meaningful to that individual. It looks like discussing a gospel question and sharing testimony to bring clarity and peace. It looks like becoming part of someone's life and caring about him or her."[16]

Similar examples were provided by other speakers at general conference.[17] We would all benefit from repeated review of those talks, which contain numerous examples of ministering that might spark the personalized revelation that must guide our efforts.

In addition to the examples provided in those inspired talks, we can find examples of inspired ministering in our everyday individual lives. If we, like Mormon, are "quick to observe" (Mormon 1:2), we will see that there are—and have been—inspired acts of ministering occurring all around us all the time.

My dear mother, now in her ninety-first year, has been a widow for more than twenty years. During most, if not all, of that time, she has received at least monthly visits from my boyhood friend Brad King. At one point I suppose Brad was assigned to my mom as her home teacher. And in that vein, through the first years, he was usually accompanied by one of his two sons. But as his sons went on missions and then moved away, Brad's visits continued, often with his wife, Tami. More important, whenever an emergency arose that distance precluded me from responding to personally, my advice to my mother was, "Call Brad." And Brad always came. Because of changes in ward boundaries, my mother lived in several different wards during that time, even though she had not moved. At some point, I was not sure that Brad was even in the same ward. But the visits continued. When my mother recently moved out of her home into an assisted living facility in another ward, Brad and Tami continued to visit regularly, at least until they left last fall to serve a mission in Hawaii. While the in-person visits have not continued due to distance, communication still occurs. What I suppose was a home teaching assignment for Brad became a simple but impactful ministering effort, motivated not by duty but by love—the kind of pure love of Christ that is at the heart of ministering. I have been inspired by Brad King's powerful example of ministering.

In the past few years, Brad's efforts have been supplemented by those of a kind family with four young children who somehow adopted my mother as their extra grandma. I don't know how the connection with the Barneys first started. They may have been in the same ward, or it may have come from my mother's visits to Brother Barney, who, as a physical therapist, had attended to her needs over the years. What I do know is that I eventually learned to avoid a certain time on Sundays for my weekly call to my mother because I knew the Barneys would be there. And I knew that as much as my mom loved talking with me, visits from the Barneys were sacred, and my calls could wait. I am grateful to the Barneys for providing such a powerful example of what holy ministering looks like.

But such ministering does not need to be so long-standing and constant in order to have an impact. Sometimes simple acts of ministering can have profound impacts because of unique circumstances. When Peggy and I moved to Provo more than thirty years ago, she came somewhat reluctantly. She had really enjoyed living in Phoenix, where we had finally settled after living in six different homes in three different cities in our short married life. She finally agreed to the move only because she knew how much a chance to teach at the BYU Law School meant to me. To compound things just a bit more, our move came only weeks after Peggy had given birth to our second son, who, due to complications, spent the first several days of his mortal life in a neonatal intensive care unit. Adding to the reluctance was the fact that we also had a very active two-year-old, who at times required full parental attention from both parents.

Within weeks after we had arrived in Provo, I was called to serve in the bishopric of a young single adult ward that met on campus. That left Peggy to attend church by herself in a ward where she didn't know anyone, accompanied only by a small infant and a very active toddler.

One particular Sunday, Peggy awoke feeling a bit over-whelmed. The prospect of going to church, chasing a two-year-old while attending to a newborn infant, and getting absolutely nothing out of the meetings except a physical workout seemed daunting. The thought came to her: *Why go?* Then came another thought—and a plan: *If I don't go at all, no one will notice. Kevin will assume that I went to the home ward, and the people in the home ward will assume I went with Kevin to the young single adult ward.*

For a moment she felt liberated. But her conscience quickly got the better of her, and she dutifully readied the children and herself and rushed off to sacrament meeting. On arriving at church, still feeling discouraged, Peggy saw Brother Larson, an older member of the ward who in the prior weeks had noticed her plight and had often silently taken our infant son to free up Peggy to chase the two-year-old. Brother Larson usually didn't say anything; he sim-ply noticed when the situation reached crisis mode, held out his arms, and received and cradled the baby. This Sunday, however, he greeted Peggy at the door, held out his arms before any crisis had started, and said five simple words: "This will be worth it."

Peggy stood there stunned as the Spirit overwhelmed her, and her attitude changed. She felt like God had sent an angel to com-fort her by saying exactly what she needed to hear. And God had. My guess is that Brother Larson had no idea of the impact he had on Peggy and on our family. But we consider him a ministering an-gel who modestly demonstrated the way small and simple inspired acts of ministry can have a profound and long-lasting impact.

If we will carefully and prayerfully observe, we will find in-spiring acts of ministry all around us. Those examples can, in turn, inspire us to act in the same way. In that regard, let me note the importance and power of ministering in ways that are not formally assigned to us. Neither Brother Larson nor the Barneys had any specific church assignment to serve, and what might have started out as a church assignment for Brad King soon transformed from a duty to a charity-driven effort to lift and love. And yet without assignments, each of these individuals blessed my loved ones and brought them closer to Christ. President M. Russell Ballard stated that we "need to be careful not to just minister to those names on a list but to minister to all of Heavenly Father's children."[18]

Another source of revelation-prompting examples of ministry is the scriptures. By my count, the terms *minister* or *ministering* appear 647 times in the scriptures. There is thus much to be learned in the scriptures about ministry. Let me cite one example. In 3 Nephi we read about Nephi, the grandson of Helaman the Younger. He would later be one of the twelve disciples chosen by Christ during His ministry in ancient America. Nephi lived at a time of great wickedness, when the people's "hearts were turned from the Lord their God" (3 Nephi 7:14.). In response, Nephi "began to testify, boldly, repentance and remission of sins through faith on the Lord Jesus Christ" (3 Nephi 7:16), as any good Church leader or missionary would.

But Nephi did more than that. As recorded in 3 Nephi 7:17, "He did minister many things unto them." And this was no ordinary ministry. According to verse 17, "Nephi did minister with power and with great authority." In the next verse we read about the remarkable effect ministering with such power and authority had on the people: "And it came to pass that . . . [the people recognized that Nephi] had greater power than they, *for it were not possible that they could disbelieve his words*" (3 Nephi 7:18; emphasis added). Nephi ministered with such power and authority that the people could not disbelieve his words. This did not mean that they all immediately joined the Church. Indeed, the record indicates that "but few . . . were converted" (3 Nephi 7:21). Most of the rest of them were just "angry with him" (3 Nephi 7:18, 20). Agency is operative in all circumstances, so our actions will not always yield the fruit that we desire. But those who chose not to respond positively to Nephi still felt the love of God so powerfully through his ministering that they could not disbelieve his words.

We might be tempted to think that ministering with such power and authority happened only in the past or that it is limited to those who are prophets and apostles. Yet in a talk tellingly entitled "Ministering with the Power and Authority of God," given during the April 2018 priesthood session, President Russell M. Nelson spoke about "faithful women [in our day] who understand the power inherent in their callings and in their endowment and other temple ordinances. These women know how to call upon the powers of heaven to protect and strengthen their husbands, their children, and others they love. These are spiritually strong women who lead, teach, and minister fearlessly in their callings with the power and authority of God!"[19]

Now I do not know exactly how one ministers with such power and authority that people cannot disbelieve what they say, but the example of Nephi is provided in the scriptures to encourage us to act on the belief that it is possible, even in our day. The scriptures abound in such insights about ministering.

Of particular significance to me in that regard are the references to Christ's ministering efforts, especially those in the Book of Mormon. Indeed, from the early part of the record to the very end, there is a focus on what that book calls Christ's ministry in the Americas.

In 1 Nephi 13, the Savior told Nephi, "I will manifest myself unto thy seed, that they shall write many things *which I shall minister unto them,* which shall be plain and precious" (1 Nephi 13:35; emphasis added). Similarly, Nephi prophesied that the remnant of Lehi's seed would "come . . . to the knowledge of the gospel of their Redeemer, *which was ministered unto their fathers by him*" (1 Nephi 15:14; emphasis added). In like manner, in 3 Nephi 10, just before beginning the record of Christ's personal visit to ancient America, Mormon noted:

"Soon after the ascension of Christ into heaven he did truly manifest himself unto them—showing his body unto them, *and ministering unto them;* and an *account of his ministry* shall be given hereafter" (3 Nephi 10:18–19; emphasis added).

Given Mormon's description and Nephi's early prophecies, everything that follows in the rest of 3 Nephi might properly be called Christ's ministering efforts among Lehi's descendants.[20] I believe we will receive increased insight into ways in which we can minister in a Christlike manner if we carefully study what Christ did and said during that particular ministry.

For example, we might note how the Savior interacted "one by one" with all those in attendance at His initial appearance (3 Nephi 11:15) and when later blessing and praying for their little children "one by one" (3 Nephi 17:21). Most, if not all, effective ministering is done one by one. The Savior Himself provided a personal example of the critical need to focus on individuals, even despite His eternally busy schedule.

Similarly, we might note the Savior's emphasis on ordinances during His ministry in ancient America. As part of His ministry, He taught about baptism (see 3 Nephi 11:22–38), He initiated the sacrament (see 3 Nephi 18:1–12), and He blessed the little children (see 3 Nephi 17:21) and others (see 3 Nephi 17:7–9). As we minister to those around us, we might profitably ask ourselves, "What ordinance do they need next in their lives?" and then think of ways in which our ministering can help them receive that ordinance, for it is only through the receipt of ordinances and the making and keeping of accompanying covenants that the ultimate end of exaltation can be achieved.

Thus I join President M. Russell Ballard in inviting you "to study 3 Nephi by identifying every reference to the word *minister* in any of its forms and every reference to the phrase one by one. Once you have thoroughly identified these words and phrases, please consider what the Book of Mormon teaches about ministering."[21]

Let me offer one additional thought suggested by the ministering example of the Savior in the scriptures—this one from the New Testament. As Jesus hung on the cross, suffering immense pain and concluding both His earthly ministry and His culminating atoning sacrifice, one of His final ministering acts was again directed at the one—in this case a special one. As recorded in John:

"When Jesus therefore saw his mother, and the disciple standing by, whom he loved, he saith unto his mother, Woman, behold thy son! Then saith he to the disciple, Behold thy mother!" (John 19:26–27).

In our earnest haste to meet the needs of all around us, let us not overlook our primary responsibility to minister in our homes and to our families. Like all the work of the Lord, the most important ministering work we "will ever do will be within the walls of [our] own homes."[22]

Once we have firmly fixed in our minds the full purpose of ministering, once we begin to inculcate in our lives the gifts of charity and the Holy Ghost, and once we have opened up revelation by observing and learning from the ministering examples of others—those living among us, and those found in the scriptures and in the teachings of our leaders—I would suggest there are yet two other things we might do (suggestions four and five) to make our ministering efforts more productive and fulfilling.

4. Unite with Others: Be One in the Work

The fourth suggestion is to recognize that our efforts will be more productive if we are united with others. This is a more unified ministering effort than we have attempted in the past. We have not only consolidated Melchizedek Priesthood quorums but are also urging and requiring more coordination, cooperation, and communication between the elders quorum and the Relief Society. And there will be more need for that same unified effort with Young Women and Aaronic Priesthood leaders as assignments are made. We will also need to think about how other efforts in areas such as missionary work, family history, and temple work can be used as tools in the ministering effort and how, conversely, ministering efforts may assist in missionary, temple, and family history work. This work will succeed in its fullest only when we are "of one heart and one mind" (Moses 7:18), as is required of the Zion people we hope to become.

That in turn will happen only as we focus on the Savior and bring people, including ourselves, unto Him. As I noted before, God is, in this dispensation, bringing all things together in one, as Paul prophesied. But He is doing so, as it says in Ephesians 1:10, by bringing all things together "in Christ."

To return to our original women's conference theme, we are to strengthen one another *in the Lord*.

5. *True Ministry Invites People to Come unto Christ*

My fifth and most important suggestion is that we always recognize and never forget that true ministering occurs only when we invite and encourage others to come unto Christ. We may temporarily meet the immediate needs of those around us, but only He can provide the living water (see John 4:14) and "the living bread" (John 6:51) that will allow them to be continually nourished in such a way that they realize their full potential as "beloved spirit son[s] or daughter[s] of heavenly parents [with] a divine nature and destiny."[23]

To succeed in our ministering, we need to bring people unto Christ. "Our charge" and "our privilege" is, as President Nelson testified, "to help prepare the world for the Second Coming of the Lord."[24] And one way to do that is by ministering in a Christlike manner. As Sister Bingham noted, "What better way to prepare to meet Him than to strive to become *like* Him through lovingly ministering to one another!"[25]

I testify that Jesus Christ lives and that He guides this Church through living prophets and through all others who will align their wills with His. He will someday return to earth to reign as King of Kings, and Lord of Lords (see Revelation 19:16). As we minister to others in His way, we will "be filled with [the] love, which [God] hath bestowed upon all who are true followers of his Son, Jesus Christ." If that happens, then "when he shall appear we shall be like him" (Moroni 7:48). May we realize that great blessing in our lives is my prayer.

Christlike Connections

Bonnie H. Cordon

I would like to focus on Christlike connections—in other words, the power and purpose that can be ours as we recognize our divine identity as daughters of God and willingly take upon ourselves the name of Jesus Christ.

Let me begin with a story—in 1993, we had moved to Indiana from the San Francisco Bay Area and I was registering Nolan, my oldest, in his new school. Tanner, my second son, wanted to go to school like his big brother. So I registered Tanner for a neighborhood preschool program. The first line of the registration asked for the *name* of the child. I wrote in "Tanner Cordon" and then proceeded to fill in all the rest of the paperwork. Tanner was excited for his first day of school. After about twenty minutes of him being in school, I received a phone call from the administration office.

"Mrs. Cordon, there seems to be a problem with your paperwork. Tanner told us his name is Tanner Buckets, not Tanner Cordon, as stated on the registration. Could you please clarify? He is quite adamant that we not call him Tanner Cordon but we use Tanner Buckets as his name." I burst into laughter.

Did my child really think his name was Tanner Buckets, the nickname my husband had given him? Had we used this name so often that he really did not know his real name? Can you guess what the topic around the dinner table was that evening? "Tanner, you are Tanner Cordon. We are all Cordons in this house." That day began our efforts to teach him what it meant to be a Cordon and what it meant to be a child of God. Identity was our key gospel topic that year.

Who are we? Are we divine? We are daughters of our Heavenly Father, who loves us! That truly is a divine identity.

We are eternally and inseparably connected to heaven and to each other. I like the way Sister Kathy Clayton said it: "We have God's spiritual DNA coursing through our veins. We are His sons and daughters and His heirs."[1]

The scriptures and the prophets teach us about our heavenly family history. We know we were with our Heavenly Parents in our premortal life. We sat in counsel and listened to our Heavenly Father's plan of happiness, the plan of salvation. We did not have physical bodies, but we had testimonies of the Savior—powerful testimonies that helped us overcome Lucifer's deception and choose to follow Heavenly Father and trust in Jesus Christ. We shouted for joy when we heard the plan and learned that we would have the chance to come to earth—this fallen earth, with all its challenges, trials, and tribulations.

Well, sisters, now we are experiencing—firsthand—our bodies and what it is like living and interacting in this fallen world. I was reminded of this quite vividly the other day. I was at a shopping mall, walking down the long, wide hall in which kiosks were placed right in the middle. A vivacious sales rep was attempting to give a small packet to every person who walked by his kiosk without much success.

I had a few spare minutes and decided to take his sample. When I reached out, he took my hand and said, "I can tell how old someone is just by looking at their hands." I thought to myself, *This is not going to end well.* He looked over my hands carefully and said, "You, ma'am, are very well-preserved for sixty-three." Sisters, I am fifty-four. I can testify we live in a fallen state—I obviously don't have perfect hands, but these hands and this body are a gift from God. To paraphrase a familiar line from the musical *Fiddler on the Roof*—"I know who I am and what God expects me to do [because of my covenants]!"[2] In 2 Nephi 31:12, we are taught, "He that is baptized in my name, to him will the Father give the Holy Ghost, like unto me; wherefore, follow me, and do the things which ye have seen me do." We are to "lift up the hands which hang down, and strengthen the feeble knees" (Doctrine and Covenants 81:5).

As President Gordon B. Hinckley taught, "Your skills are needed, whatever they may be. Your helping hands will lift someone out of the mire of distress. Your steady voice will give encouragement to some who might otherwise simply give up. Your skills can change the lives, in a remarkable and wonderful way, of those who walk in need. If not now, when? If not you, who?"[3]

So what did the Savior do during His mortal ministry? How did He fulfill His earthly mission? What Christlike example is ours to follow? Let's look at some attributes that illustrate His life—and if you're like me, when you see these beautiful Christlike connections, some will speak to your heart. I invite you to pay attention to that spiritual nudge.

As we choose to live our covenants and follow our Savior, here are just a few things we can do:

Feed the hungry

Lift those who suffer

Cherish His little ones

Listen

Invite growth

Honor parents

Seek to understand

Counsel together

Nurture

Ask for help

Serve with priesthood power

Acknowledge others

Give comfort

Gather together

Give new life

Involve and prepare others

Walk with

Instill confidence

Guide

Recognize the contributions of others

Forgive

Defend truth

Mourn with those that mourn

Seek those who are lost

Give new sight

Teach

Witness

Calm the storms

Sustain those who hold priesthood keys

Show patience

Make and keep covenants

Encourage love

Offer hope

We could spend days exploring this list, but I want to share examples of just a few faithful individuals who are striving to make Christlike connections and give Christlike service.

GIVE NEW LIFE

This is a bold place to begin, but here goes . . .

In the October 2017 general conference, Sister Joy D. Jones shared the story of Taiana, a young woman who fought a brave battle against cancer for eighteen months.[4] Sister Jones and I had the chance to visit her just before she passed away. We sang songs and rejoiced in the short, brief life of this remarkable young woman.

Before she passed, Taiana had completed about 500 family names for the temple. Every Saturday she faithfully went to do baptisms for the dead, and almost every weekend she would host a "family history party." Her mother shared that she recently had a strong feeling to look at Taiana's phone. She clicked on a small file out of curiosity, and lo and behold, there were forty-nine temple-ready names. They had been found and researched by Taiana but she was too sick to print them out for temple work.

August 2018 will mark the one-year anniversary of Taiana's passing. Her family and friends will be in the temple continuing her effort to bring people to Christ on both sides of the veil.

We may not have the power to raise the dead like our Savior, but I truly believe we can give new life to those beyond the veil as we participate in temple and family history work.

SHOW PATIENCE

Following the Saturday afternoon session of the April 2018 general conference, Sister Becky Craven and I wanted to show her family her new office. On our way there, my daughter said she was not feeling well and would just lie down in my car and wait until we were done—I was her ride home. We were there for a good space of time. When I arrived back to the car, Heather was still very sick but she did not say anything about the wait time. On the way to drop her off, we used a bag that was (thankfully) in the car for her to throw up her lunch. She was sick. As we dropped her off, my daughter-in-law Hana commented, "Wow, what service! She never complained even though she was so sick." What a kind and Christlike gift of time and patience she gave to me.

GIVE NEW SIGHT

In April 2018, a remarkable family in northern Utah lost their son in a tragic accident. They struggled to find solace. Peace seemed impossible. An inspired friend came to visit. He brought love and reminded them of truths they had forgotten in their anguish as he offered this example.

He said that in the countless times he and his wife have attended the temple, no matter how hard they try to time it just right, they have never entered the celestial room at the same time—as one of them inevitably arrives before the other. He related this example to our individual departures from this mortal realm to the other side of the veil.

This gentle insight renewed their gratitude for the plan of happiness and brought fresh perspective. It gave them a glimmer of light in their dark world, a beacon of hope they have gone back to again and again as they slowly make their way toward the promise of brighter days. Can your efforts to share your faith bring light, hope, and new sight to those in darkness?

LIFT THOSE WHO SUFFER

Like my daughter, most of us have become very good at hiding our suffering from the world, not wanting to burden others. This is why we need that heavenly connection—that inspiration that comes from the Holy Ghost to help us know who needs us. A new friend shared this example: "My goal is to improve my ability to hear and respond to the promptings of the Holy Ghost. I have most certainly failed more often than I have succeeded— but one day I got it right. I kept thinking of a friend. My first thought was, *I haven't seen Deb in a while; I should make cookies and take them over to her.* Again, her name came to my mind. I finally abandoned my traditional treat and just picked up the phone. I was surprised when my casual greeting was met with tears. She had received some difficult news about her pregnancy and just needed a listening ear and word of encouragement."

Cookies are nice, but better still is a timely response to the Spirit and a simple call or text to reach out in a moment of need.

It really is as simple as the Savior showed us; He "went about doing good" (Acts 10:38)—and so can we! And by becoming the answer to someone's prayer, we often find the answer to our own. As taught by President Spencer W. Kimball, "The more we serve our fellowmen in appropriate ways, the more substance there is to our souls."[5] Christlike connections may bless others, but I can promise that you will be forever changed!

Sisters, we have a divine identity, and with it comes a divine purpose and responsibility to serve, to connect with others as our Savior would, to be His hands. Our prophet, President Russell M.

Nelson, has pleaded with us as covenant-keeping women, "My dear sisters, [we] need your strength, your conversion, your conviction, your ability to lead, your wisdom, and your voices."[6]

My dear friends, let's accept this invitation to act. "Let us cheerfully do all things that lie in our power; and then may we stand still, with the utmost assurance, to see the salvation of God, and for his arm to be revealed" (Doctrine and Covenants 123:17).

"Love One Another, as I Have Loved You"

Jennifer Brinkerhoff Platt

I'd like to tell you about a recent trip to the grocery store. (Our favorite thing, of course.) As I was driving to the store, I called my husband to unload. I was feeling overwhelmed, exhausted, and spent. One more demand on my time and I was going to snap. We were out of everything: money, groceries, and time. But I needed to feed my family and I had thirty free minutes, so the grocery store it was. My two-year-old boy and I headed there together and started a very deliberate shopping trip. I began to feel myself calm down just a little as I started to engage with my son, narrating everything and asking questions. "Nelson, where is the bread? How about the peas? How about the soy sauce—why can't we find the soy sauce?" It seemed like we had been looking forever—why was the soy sauce so hard to find? We had been looking forever, and as we began to turn down one aisle, a woman approached me. She said, "The soy sauce is right there." It was just around the corner in the next aisle. And then she looked at me—I think she was probably a little embarrassed because she thought, *How would I know she needed soy sauce?*— and she said, "I heard you ask where it was."

I felt so grateful. It was truly a moving experience for me. Such a simple gesture—did she know I was rushed and frenzied and anxious to get this task done? "Thank you!" I said. Next, we saw a man giving out sample cookies. Now, I don't care how big of a hurry you're in, there is always time for a sample cookie! We stopped and we indulged, and then we headed straight to the cheese. As we got to the cheese section, the cookie man approached me and I thought, *Great, what does he want?* He said, "I'm about to end my shift." Oh, no, he needs a ride. I don't have time for this. Thirty minutes, that's all I've got, and I've got to get out of here, and by this time, I didn't even have that. I was not in a charitable state of mind. I couldn't manage one more thing, not one more request. Now, imagine my embarrassment when he looked at me and said instead, "These cookies are paid for. My shift is ending; I'm not going to get rid of all of them. Can I give you a package?" Turns out they're *Mother's* Cookies! My eyes filled with tears. "Of course I'll take your cookies. Thank you!" (And you better believe I'm going to eat every one of them!) We followed him back to his little display table so he could put a smiley face sticker on it to prove I didn't steal them. And as he handed me the package, I had the presence of mind to feel this impression, an invitation to stop.

"My name is Jennifer," I said to him, "and it's been a rough day."

"I'm George, and I thought so."

"Thank you, George, for lightening my burden in such a simple way." Then he told me something really important about himself.

"You know," he began, "my dad taught me to do things like this. Growing up we always had extra kids living in our house.

My dad was always finding someone that he noticed who needed a kindness; that's just the kind of person he was. He died recently and I want to honor him." I hugged George and left for the milk, and thanked him for doing things in remembrance of his father.

In a matter of seconds, I was transformed. Changed. Filled with hope, and peace, and joy in the Holy Ghost. I had found the love of Jesus Christ in the grocery store.

In a small way, I feel I have come to know you through this process. I've come to know a bit of your heaviness. Your burdens. The weight you carry and the hope you're seeking. The Spirit we desire. Not because I know each of you individually, but because I know Jesus Christ. He's shown you to me these past months as I've prepared for this moment. We need the Spirit. We need Jesus Christ. His invitation is to come unto Him and to join Him in His work. I plead for the gift and power of the Holy Ghost for each one of us, to know and understand His role as a special ministering messenger, and to also know our own purpose. My hope is that each of us will feel custom messages just for us. That these messages will give us clarity about our own personal ministries and teach us how to love one another as Jesus Christ loves us. I pray that we will have the courage to act on what we receive today.

Jesus Christ's entire life—premortal, mortal, and post-mortal—is a ministry of love. Pure love. Charity. We experience and understand His love in so many ways. Perhaps few scriptural accounts more sacredly illustrate His love than what we find in the gospel of John, particularly during His final days. Will you come with me to a sacred space? To an upper room. A space elevated and separate from the noise of the world. Let's leave behind the busyness of the city preparing for a Passover feast. Come with Christ, who knows heavy burdens. "Father," He says, "save me from this hour: but for this cause came I unto this hour. Father, glorify thy name . . ." (John 12:27–28). And so we gather, you and I, as His disciples. Imagine, if you can, the Lord, kneeling before you. He's "laid aside his garments; and took a towel, and girded himself. After that he poureth water into a basin, and began to wash the disciples' feet, and to wipe them with the towel where-with he was girded" (John 13:4–5). Maybe we feel like Peter:

"Thou needest not to wash my feet. Jesus answered him, If I wash thee not, thou hast no part with me. Simon Peter saith unto him, Lord, not my feet only, but also my hands and my head. Jesus saith to him, He that has washed his hands and his head, needeth not save to wash his feet, but is clean every whit; and ye are clean" (JST, John 12:8–10).

We, like Peter, desire to be clean, every whit. Together we partake of the emblems of His flesh. Bread—each piece unique and different, just like you and me. Wine—the symbol of the blood He was about to shed.[1]

We feel the power of the symbols. Unity. Purification. Spiritual power. And like the disciples He has tutored and trusted, we need the Holy Ghost. Because Christ is not with us right now, He has prepared His trusted friends. They are quali-fied, these eleven men, who would suffer in remembrance of Him in their apostolic mortal ministries.

"A new commandment I give unto you, That ye love one an-other; as I have loved you, that ye also love one another. By this shall all men know that ye are my disciples, if ye have love one to another" (John 13:34).

Even Peter struggled with figuring out how to pursue this higher, holier command. Christ cautioned him, "Behold, Satan hath desired to have you, that he may sift you as wheat: but I have prayed for thee, that thy faith fail not: and when thou art converted, strengthen thy brethren" (Luke 22:31–32).

There is a pattern in this. None of us are exempt from Satan and his desire to deceive us. He wants sifting to destroy us. Christ, however, wants sifting to convert and refine us. Think about it. Do you ever have a recipe that calls for sifted flour? If you're like me, you skip the step. You don't have time, or you don't have a sifter, or you don't care. Or you don't really understand why it matters. Yet sifting refines, purifies, and breaks down coarseness—or natural-man tendencies—to produce a better-quality bread. Even living bread.[2] We become converted or changed as we experience the siftings of the adversary, and we can trust that Christ continues to pray for us.

"I pray not that thou shouldest take them out of the world, but that thou shouldest keep them from the evil" (John 17:15).

You and I can learn to resist evil by following Christ's pattern. This pattern includes trying to love one another as He loves us. This is a process of unity—becoming *one* with Jesus Christ and the Father as we seek to minister to others one by one, just as He does.

I want to share with you a few observations of Christ's pattern of love. I'll focus on three principles. The first is this: Christ makes the ordinary sacred, and so can we. Two, Christ teaches us to understand doctrine. And three, He prepares us to receive the Holy Ghost.

THE ORDINARY BECOMES SACRED

Let's begin by focusing on this first point, the ordinary becoming sacred. I want to teach you something that has helped me to learn to love others as Christ does. It helps me get out of the monotony and find possibilities for love—even in grocery stores. This is something I learned in my doctoral studies while

I was working in Ethiopia. I was drawn to Ethiopia when I was thirteen years old. If you're old enough, you might remember the desperate situation that we saw on television in the 1980s. In fact, there was a lot of fundraising that happened during that time to help people in Africa. Do you remember the song *We Are the World*? There was also a Church-wide fast in 1985 under the direction of President Spencer W. Kimball. That fast was amazing. Members of the Church gave so many offerings that the prophet asked Presiding Bishop Glen Pace and President M. Russell Ballard to travel to Ethiopia and figure out how to distribute the $6 million donated by members of the Church. Their experiences were remarkable, and they sought to offer relief to those suffering.[3]

Something about all of this appealed to my young-girl soul. Even more so, I think that the Holy Ghost was preparing me for some eventual work in this glorious country. I really do believe that each of us has a specific mission and ministry to perform on this earth. It's unique to each of us and discovered over and over throughout our lifetime in revelatory bursts and quiet whisperings.

Fast-forward from 1985 to 2008. I was drawn to earn a PhD. God calls us to do specific things, and sometimes they're hard and scary, but when we know they are from Him, we can do anything; that was how I felt about earning a PhD. When we tune our hearts to hear His voice, He'll speak, and direct, and lead us in paths that we "know not, save the Lord commanded me" (Moses 5:6). In the summer of 2009, I went to Ethiopia to initiate my doctoral studies. I gave people cameras and said, "I want you to show me what it looks like to live your life—take photos from the moment you wake up until you go to bed at night. Then come back and bring those photos to me and we'll look through them together to identify some patterns." As I would comb through all of these photographs, every one of them showed me the same event: the Ethiopian coffee ceremony.[4] This became the focus of my research. I wanted to understand how the Ethiopian coffee ceremony, or *Buna*, helped to shape female identity. Little did I know that this would shape the rest of my life.

My Ethiopian friends laugh at me every time I tell them how passionate I am about coffee because they say, "You've never even tasted it." But imagine this: What would it be like for you to gather with your closest friends and neighbors every day, sometimes more than once a day, just to love each other? That is Buna. Everything stops for Buna.

Most every day my mind wanders to a dusty village in Ethiopia—Dera. I catch myself longing to be surrounded by my beautiful friends. I can smell the smoke of incense and fire, roasting beans—coffee. Buna. I long to be in a sacred circle of sisters. They gather to talk. To escape life. To drink coffee. To love.

When my heart wants to be there, I imagine watching them. Listening. Learning. I see them prepare. One woman, the hostess, takes the lead in preparing the coffee. Grinding, boiling, then serving. The women participate in a variety of ways. Many women have brought their babies or young children with them. They tend to them while participating. Others have brought work to do. Handwork or sewing. And some have just taken a break. Each woman is welcome. Safe. Included. Loved. They eat popcorn or other snacks, trying to prolong their Buna experience, and eventually the Jebena pot is empty and they go back to work, whatever that work is. Filled. Content. Buoyed up. Remembering their time together. Thinking about each other. Wishing for the next Buna circle to come quickly.

When I asked the women about their ritual, they would say to me, "Well, this is just something that we do. Our mothers did it. Our daughters will do it. Buna is part of our lives." An Ethiopian friend of mine who now lives in the United States tells me, "If I have a problem, we don't have those psychiatry or something to tell us what to do, so that's the way we treat each other, you know? If I have a problem, we just talk about it and the other ladies tell you a solution."[5] In a natural, organic way, my Ethiopian friends just take care of each other. There is no need for an appointment, an invitation; they gather, and they minister.

Like my Ethiopian friends, we often do good and important things that feel ordinary and routine. As an outsider, it was easy for me to see how special and unique this context is. And truly, if you know an Ethiopian woman, she really does value her Buna time. But here's what was so transforming to me: I realized that when we do the things we claim to value with the intent of making them sacred, we feel the love of the Lord in our lives. Buna is a ritual, an act performed with great intention. Looking at the lives of someone so different from me helped me to see that I likewise do ordinary things but often get caught in the monotony of them, forgetting that we—you and me—can live intentional, focused lives without adding to our already busy schedules. Rather, we can simply do those ordinary things on purpose. We can ritualize our lives.[6]

Here's how I have learned to define ritual—it's really pretty simple. It is making something sacred or holy. If I were to make a study of your life, the things you do from the time you wake in the morning until you go to bed at night, what one or two things would I observe that you consistently do? Make your bed? Drive the carpool? Go to work?

What would it look like to make that one thing sacred? Holy? Dedicated or consecrated to God? Let's use my trip to the grocery store as an example. I was in a bad state of mind. But with the help of my kind husband and the Holy Ghost, I realized I could ritualize the experience.

Now, it's important to note that there are three simple components to ritualizing something—you may even have noticed them as I was describing Buna. First, we prepare, then we participate, and then we remember. It's that simple. It's just a matter of doing it. And trust me, choosing to ritualize the ordinary things we do really does help us not only to feel the Savior's love for us, but to extend it to others.

I prepared for the grocery store by making a list. I also decided to be present with my son. I wanted to really focus on him. We had this half hour for just the two of us to be alone, so I wanted to engage with him. I was also hoping being present with him would be a much-needed break from the craziness of the day.

Then I participated in the shopping process. I not only wanted to, I *needed* to feel Christ's love for me. I know that may sound odd to you. "Gee, I think I'll go to the grocery store so I can feel loved." But I needed to feel love so badly in those moments, and I wanted to hope I'd feel it by simply being with other people. All I had time for was getting groceries. The shopping needed to be done. You may not have felt the Holy Ghost the last time someone helped you find soy sauce on aisle ten. Or while sampling a cookie. Those experiences may not have affected you the way they did me. But they were impactful because I needed them to be. I was participating in my process.

Christ speaks love to us through the Holy Ghost whenever we ask for it. And it is absolutely in the ordinary. This is Christ's pattern. His whole life was spent loving people where they were, and you better believe He didn't leave them there. He lifted and elevated them to a higher, holier place. He used bread, fish, and lilies to teach profound doctrines. He healed while walking dusty streets, and He loved always.

So we participate in our lives with great intention, focusing on Him.

The last part of the ritual process, after we've prepared and participated, is to remember. Sometimes remembering is simply evaluating what happened and asking ourselves, "What would I do differently?" Or, in moments like this conference, it's remembering how good it felt.

Is there something you'd like to ritualize in your life? The way you drive to work? Or the way you make your bed? How about your prayers? I really believe that we can feel the power of loving as Christ loves by laying our hearts on the altar and making a whole-soul offering to Him as we pray.

"And now, my beloved [sisters], I would that ye should come unto Christ, who is the Holy One of Israel, and partake of his salvation, and the power of his redemption. Yea, come unto him, and offer your whole souls as an offering unto him, and continue in fasting and prayer, and endure to the end; and as the Lord liveth ye will be saved" (Omni 1:26).

How do we make a whole-soul offering? We give Him our heart, might, mind, and strength—we hold nothing back. And I believe that begins with prayer—earnest, intentional, sacred prayer that takes so much work. We prepare for prayer by thinking and pondering about our desires. This includes blessings we desire both for ourselves and others.[7] We may even write these things down. We prepare by finding a sacred, secret place. What else do you do to prepare yourself to pray? I hope you'll think about it and start to make a plan to be ready to pray.

Then we kneel and participate as we unite ourselves with the Father, the Son, and the Holy Ghost. Isn't that extraordinary and significant? To commune with the Godhead? We seek His will, just like Christ in His great intercessory prayer, and we account for our stewardships.

"I have glorified thee on the earth: I have finished the work which thou gavest me to do" (John 17:4).

We aren't finished yet, so we ask for help. Are my offerings acceptable? What would thou have me do? What if, like Jesus, we asked to have a sense for who we were in the premortal world— who we've always been?

"O Father, glorify thou me with thine own self with the glory which I had with thee before the world was" (John 17:5).

In prayer, we can seek for truth.

"Sanctify them through thy truth: thy word is truth" (John 17:17).

We seek for unity.

"That they all may be one; as thou, Father, art in me, and I in thee, that they also may be one in us: that the world may believe that thou hast sent me" (John 17:21).

Make us one, we plead. We plead for the power of His redemption, and we seek to make a whole-soul offering.

And then we remember. We remember the promptings, the feelings, the ideas that all come to us in the act of prayer. And then we act in faith. We pray always, hoping to feel the Holy Ghost with us guiding us as we grow, stretch, and act in His love.

A friend of mine shared with me her experience in this kind of prayer. Read her words as she expresses a whole-soul offering:

"My largest experience with feeling God's love came not in a moment when I felt the most stable in my faith. No, it came when I accepted who I was and stopped pretending to be someone I was not. Growing up and knowing that I was gay and Mormon caused a lot of anxiety, shame, and fear. Fear that there really was something wrong with me, that I really was evil, a monster even. That I didn't have a plan of salvation. Like many, I prayed countless times that if God would just take this away, I would do anything. However, my attraction grew and solidified, and the years went on, and I started to believe that maybe God hated me. I did not believe I was worthy of love or happiness.

"One night, I was exhausted and felt I had hit rock bottom. I knelt beside my bed, shaking. I remembered Joseph Smith kneeling in the grove. He asked a simple question. Why couldn't I?

"So I knelt—a final effort to see if someone was really there. I prayed, 'Dear Father, I'm gay. Are you okay with that?' As I paused, an overwhelming peace covered me, such as I had not felt in many, many years. It almost felt as if someone was hugging me. Then, crystal clear in my mind, these powerfully calm words came: 'I know. And I love you.'

"In that moment, with incredible clarity, I realized that God had never abandoned me. God never hated me. In hiding myself and allowing shame to overcome me, there was no room to feel God's love. In that moment when I accepted who I was, I could feel God's love again and I started to recognize the Spirit more readily. I felt joy for the first time in years and, most importantly, I felt compassion and love for those around me too. No matter how difficult or complicated life gets, we are always worthy of happiness and love–especially the love of the Good Shepherd."[8]

I love my friend. I love her courage and the way she offers her whole soul to the Lord, not just in mighty prayer, but in the way she lives. That mighty prayer has led her to the temple, where she has made covenants with our God. She knows her divine identity and her worth.

When we try to make an offering to the Lord, we shouldn't hold anything back. After all, He already knows. And somehow in our expression of our deepest desires, hurts, fears, and joys, we feel more sure of how He feels. I know that the Holy Ghost bears powerful witness to each of our broken and malleable hearts that we are absolutely exquisite in His eyes. We are divine. And He needs us to know it and own it. We are loved and cherished and absolutely adored by the creator of heaven and earth. And when we know that, we love others as He does. Being purposeful in our lives helps us to love one another as He loves us. And He does love us!

DOCTRINE

Another thing that helps us to love others as Christ does, the second point, is to seek to understand His love doctrinally. What is the doctrine of love? Rather than just state what others have taught the doctrine of love to be, I'm going to teach you an approach to discover for yourself. We need to do this by differentiating between *doctrines*, *principles*, and *applications*. Let me pause for a moment to witness to you the power that comes to our lives when we learn to not only understand doctrine, but to act in it. The doctrine of Christ is so pure, so obtainable, and so necessary to us becoming who He needs us to be. Further, we live in a world that claims a Christ who is permissible and accepting of all behaviors. While Christ's love is "perfect, infinite, enduring, and universal,"[9] His laws and standards cannot be violated if we really want to experience and understand divine love.

After all, we know that "when we obtain any blessing from God, it is by obedience to that law upon which it is predicated" (Doctrine and Covenants 130:21). "I, the Lord, am bound when you do what I say; but when ye do not what I say, ye have no promise" (Doctrine and Covenants 82:10). And we know that the Lord has said, "If ye love me, keep my commandments" (John 14:15).

Any effort we make to understand divine love for ourselves empowers us against false ideologies about Christ. When we understand His doctrine, we know how to love each other and come to Him to be refined and perfected.

To illustrate how to understand and seek His doctrine, I want to use a methodology that Elder David A. Bednar teaches.[10] He teaches us how to distinguish between doctrines, principles, and applications. They really are different from one another. While we may talk or teach that they are the same thing, they're not. So let's get clear on what they are.

Doctrine is eternal truth. It is given to us from God through prophets. These eternal truths point us to Jesus Christ. Doctrines are unchanging and relatively few in number. Doctrines answer the question of *why.* Some examples of doctrine—and these will be familiar I hope—are the Godhead, the plan of salvation, Jesus Christ and His Atonement, prophets and revelation, ordinances and covenants, the family, and commandments. These are the basic doctrines of our youth curriculum.[11] It's worth our every effort to study and know these doctrines.

Now, consider how principles are different from doctrines. Principles are also eternal truths, but they guide us to know *how* to use doctrine. Like doctrine, they are unchanging, but they answer the question *what*. *What* should I do to act in doctrine?

Often, we hear principles stated as *if-then* statements,[12] the classic being, "Inasmuch as ye shall keep my commandments, ye shall prosper in the land."[13] Obedience becomes an important principle for living the doctrine of commandments. Likewise, the Word of Wisdom is a principle with a promise which helps us to honor our bodies. The doctrine of the body is central to the plan of salvation. We utilize our agency to live the principle so that we can be healthy and free from bad habits and addiction. Honoring our body helps us to feel and experience the doctrine of the Holy Ghost more profoundly in our lives. The Spirit helps us to prepare to live with God again. How many doctrines did you find in living that one principle of the Word of Wisdom?

Applications, then, vary broadly. They are received individually and through the Spirit. Applications help us to know *how* we should act in doctrine.

I want to repeat that applications are very personal and customized—they are unique to individuals. Understanding this is important, because we often compare how we live with how others do. But if we really understand the distinction between doctrines, principles, and applications, then we will work to focus more on the doctrine—the *why* of our behaviors—rather than *how* we each apply that doctrine in our lives. Focusing on application or *how* we live is divisive. I shouldn't judge you for what the Holy Ghost is telling you to do. I may not understand your approach, but if we are one in doctrine, in the *why*, then it doesn't matter how we pursue living that doctrine as long as we are striving to follow the Spirit.

Observing the Sabbath day is a great example. Remember

when Christ healed a man on the Sabbath day? The Jews were concerned, and they even persecuted Jesus. They sought to slay Him because He had healed on the Sabbath day. "But Jesus answered them, My Father worketh hitherto, and I work. Therefore the Jews sought the more to kill him, because he not only had broken the sabbath, but said also that God was his Father, making himself equal with God" (John 5:17–18).

The Jews were caught up in *how* the Sabbath was observed, not *why*. In contrast, from the beginning to the end of His mortal life, Christ was always focused on the Father and being one with Him:

"And this is life eternal, that they might know thee the only true God, and Jesus Christ, whom thou hast sent. I have glorified thee on the earth: I have finished the work which thou gavest me to do" (John 17:3–5).

Continually aligning ourselves with the doctrine helps us to be one in Christ as He is one with the Father. Think of the love we extend to each other when instead of judging *how* another person is living, we assume the very best—that they are pursuing doctrine. Look for and trust the *why* of others' behaviors. Teach and testify of *why* we do what we do. When we do this, we gain entrance into the sacred spaces of one another's hearts, where there is hidden sorrow that the eye can't see.[14] We also learn to pursue our questions differently and find peace with some of the ambiguity associated with mortality.

It takes a lot of work, patience, and time to train ourselves to be doctrinally focused. But we can use this simple rubric: *Doctrines* answer the *why*; *principles* answer *what*; and *applications* teach *how* to press forward in this glorious cause.

President Boyd K. Packer said:

"True doctrine, understood, changes attitudes and behaviors. The study of the doctrines of the gospel will improve behavior quicker than a study of behavior will improve behavior. Preoccupation with unworthy behavior can lead to unworthy behavior. That is why we stress so forcefully the study of the doctrines of the gospel."[15]

Or, stated another way, the study of the *why* of the gospel will improve *how* we live the gospel quicker than studying *how* we live the gospel.

So what behavior do you want to change so that you can love others the way Christ does?

Think about it. What holds you back from loving fully? Maybe it's needing to forgive someone who has wronged you? Repenting of a favorite little sin? Or learning to really own and embrace your divine identity? Rather than focusing on behaviors that might change those ideas, we study the doctrine, learn the *why* behind what we're trying to change, then patiently pursue that change. We can discover and understand the doctrine, then be intentional in watching for the miracles that follow.

The Holy Ghost will tell you *how* you should act. With a little time and effort, you'll start to see doctrines everywhere. When we find ourselves in a sticky, or confusing, or uncertain situation, go to the doctrine. Ask yourself, *what is the doctrine* I need to understand to help me to see the *why* of this situation?

Do you see how this helps us to get past checklists, reports, or a task-oriented mentality to really be able to live an intentional life? Doctrine helps us to see a higher and holier way to live in this mortal realm so we can live with Jesus Christ and the Father again. To live with them once more[16] should be an ultimate *why* for each of us.

This leads me to the energy we're feeling in this conference, in general conference, in talking about the recent changes that have been announced, and the new approaches and invitations for us to serve one another, the changes in quorums, and the inclusion of young women in holy ministering work. But *why* are these changes happening? Why is President Russell M. Nelson receiving this revelation for the Church right now?

He needs us to be ready for Christ's return. Christ is coming back. President Nelson invited the men of the Church to literally stand up, rise with him, and commit to be united as men of God. He said:

"Think of your duty as God's mighty army to help prepare the world for the Second Coming of the Lord. This is our charge. This is our privilege."[17]

Sisters, it is our charge and it is our privilege to arise! Look to Jesus Christ and respond to the plea of a prophet to have a bedrock understanding of Christ's doctrine:

"Attacks against the Church, its doctrine, and our way of life are going to increase. Because of this, we need women who have a bedrock understanding of the doctrine of Christ and who will use that understanding to teach and help raise a sin-resistant generation. We need women who can detect deception in all of its forms. We need women who know how to access the power that God makes available to covenant keepers and who express their beliefs with confidence and charity. We need women who have the courage and vision of our Mother Eve.

"My dear sisters, nothing is more crucial to your eternal life than your own conversion. It is converted, covenant-keeping women—and I include my dear wife Wendy—whose righteous lives will increasingly stand out in a deteriorating world and who will thus be seen as different and distinct in the *happiest* of ways."[18]

We can do this! We are doing this already, responding to the plea of our prophet. We can align ourselves with our prophet, President Russell M. Nelson, acting in doctrine as we minister one by one. We are promised miracles. Think of the doctrine of prophets and revelation as taught by Ammon in the Book of Mormon:

"A seer is a revelator and a prophet also; and a gift which is greater can no man have, except he should possess the power of God, which no man can. Yet a man may have great power given him from God. But a seer can know of things which are past, and also of things which are to come, and by them shall all things be revealed . . . Thus God has provided a means that man, through faith, might work mighty miracles; therefore he becometh a great benefit to his fellow beings" (Mosiah 8:16–18).

President Russell M. Nelson is a great benefit to us. We can experience mighty miracles by standing with him and doing our part. Don't worry if what you do looks different from what someone else does. Remember, comparing ourselves to others is focusing on the *how* of acting in doctrine. Use your gifts and talents and abilities to build the kingdom right where you are. We don't have to be the president of anything to do good things. In fact, the least among us can become the greatest ministers.

When I served as my ward Primary president a few years ago, I suggested that we call a woman with Down's syndrome named Virginia as a Primary worker. The bishopric was hesitant. Though nearly fifty years old, Virginia had never had a Church calling. Would this be the right one or the right time?

I persisted. Virginia was called as a Primary worker, and her specific calling was to love the children. In a letter to her and then later, in a simple orientation, I explained that I felt the Lord had called her to love, whatever that meant to her. Some Sundays she would sit among the children and sing her heart out. Other Sundays she would stand with me at the door to greet the children as they entered. I would often say the name of the child to welcome them so she would know their names.

"Hello, Susan. Welcome to Primary today," I would say.

Then Virginia would often compliment the child or take their face in her hands and draw them near and say, "Hello, Susan. I love you."

There was a purity she brought to us as she nurtured and ministered one by one not just to the children, but to all of us. I'll never forget the day when Virginia took a nearly eight-year-old boy's face in her hands, looked into his eyes and said: "I love you." After a few seconds, he turned back to me and said: "Sister Platt, what am I feeling?"

I told him he was feeling the Holy Ghost, borne to him through love.

I miss Virginia every single Sunday. Especially when we sing her favorite songs. I long for her to hold me tight and tell me, "I love you!"

You see, the *why* for her was clear. She was a special messenger from Jesus Christ on this earth. We were blessed to know this miraculous and pure soul. And I'd like to believe she's with us here. Virginia, I love you.

What's your *why*? Can you ritualize it by preparing, participating, and remembering in such a way that you make it sacred and holy to you? Try to make it matter by being intentional and purposeful, acting in remembrance of our Savior, Jesus Christ.

I was so moved by George, the cookie guy at the grocery store, and his expression to me as he tried to serve others in remembrance of his father. He wants to remember his dad, and so he thinks about him and tries to do the kind of good that he saw his dad do. Let us each try to do the kind of good that Christ does, as Christ remembers His Father.

When we come to know Jesus Christ, not just socially or culturally but doctrinally, we know how to love as He loves. We are protected because we aren't worrying about how other people live but want to be unified in *why* we press forward. What will this look like in your life today? Tomorrow? In the coming weeks or months? What commitments is the Holy Ghost asking you to make so that, together, we can act in doctrine in a unified sisterhood? Christ wants us to know his doctrine.

THE HOLY GHOST

My third point is how Christ prepares us to receive the Holy Ghost. In the upper room, Peter asked, "Lord, whither goest thou? Jesus answered him, Whither I go, thou canst not follow me now; but thou shalt follow me afterwards. Peter said unto him, Lord, why cannot I follow thee now? I will lay down my life for thy sake" (John 13:36–37).

To lay down our lives for Christ's sake is to surrender our will. It's learning to want what He wants us to want, and being willing to be inconvenienced or stretched when there doesn't seem to be anything more to give. It's the Holy Ghost saying, *Stop and talk to the cookie guy.* And it's the miracle of the two fishes and five loaves that continues for each of us every day when we give Him our heart and our will. Laying down our lives looks like planning your day and then being open to others' disruptions—knocking at the door and needing you *right then*—even though you're diligently trying to work on your to-do list.

But we can only lay down our lives under the direction of the Holy Ghost. Our covenant promise to have the Holy Ghost as a constant companion should be taken at face value. Learning to recognize and receive the Holy Ghost is vital. What does that look like for you? How does the Holy Ghost talk to you? What does it feel like? What have been the patterns of revelation throughout your life? When do you notice a void of the Spirit in your life? It's important to make a study of these things and understand how the Holy Ghost communicates with each of us.

Christ taught His disciples and us, "I will pray the Father, and he shall give you another Comforter, that he may abide with you for ever; even the Spirit of truth; whom the world cannot receive, because it seeth him not, neither knoweth him: but ye know him; for he dwelleth with you, and shall be in you" (John 14:16–17).

"But the Comforter, which is the Holy Ghost, whom the Father will send in my name, he shall teach you all things, and bring all things to your remembrance, whatsoever I have said unto you. Peace I leave with you, my peace I give unto you: not as the world giveth, give I unto you. Let not your heart be troubled, neither let it be afraid" (John 14:26–27).

We can commit to seeking to understand, feel, and act on the promptings of the Holy Ghost. And we can experience peace in Christ. He will lead us to do things in small and simple ways. We can commit to love as Christ loves and strive to leave others filled with the Spirit when they have been with us. This can happen by simply learning to hold our souls still and observe.

My friend Cori tells a wonderful family story that illustrates how we can lift and elevate others in the simplest of ways:

"One Sunday afternoon our family gathered around our big oak table for dinner. Soon my daughter Kate's laughter rose above the talk. 'Gram, you're silly!' she said. We all turned to see my mom delicately lifting to her mouth a small strand of peas on the blade of her knife. All but one pea made it, and everyone clapped. Then Mom told us the story behind her unorthodox technique:

"'When I was little we didn't have much. It was the Depression. But we did have a table full of food because my father grew wonderful vegetables. Lots of hobos who had jumped onto the train wandered into our property, looking for a meal. More often than not an extra seat was pulled up to our dinner table.'

"'One summer afternoon I was sweeping the kitchen floor when my father's voice came through the screen door: "Lizzy, set another plate. We have company tonight." Our guest paused in the doorway, and dipped his head in a gesture of gratitude. "Looks like he doesn't speak much English," Dad said, "but he's hungry like we are, and his name is Henry."'

"'When dinner was ready Henry stood until we were all seated, then gently perched on the edge of his chair, his head bowed and his hat in his lap. The blessing was said and dishes were passed from hand to hand.'

"'We all waited, as was proper, for our guest to take the first bite. Henry must have been so hungry he didn't notice us watching him as he grabbed his knife. Carefully he slid the blade into the pile of peas before him, and then lifted a quivering row to his mouth without spilling a single pea. He was eating with his knife! I looked at my sister May and we covered our mouths to muffle our snickers. Henry took another knife-full, and then another.'

"'My father, taking note of the glances we were exchanging, firmly set down his fork. He looked me in the eye, then took his knife and thrust it into the peas on his plate. Most of them fell off as he attempted to lift them to his mouth, but he continued until all the peas were gone.'

"'Dad never did use his fork that night, because Henry didn't. It was one of my father's silent lessons in acceptance. He understood the need of this man to maintain his dignity, to feel comfortable in a strange place with people of different customs. Even at my young age I understood the greatness of my father's simple act of brotherhood.'

"Mom paused, looked at her grandchildren, and winked as she plowed her knife into a mountain of peas."[19]

The Holy Ghost will help us to see how we can extend Christlike love in ordinary moments. We feel peace, clarity, and joy when we respond to the nudges of the Spirit. It isn't always easy or comfortable to act, but the results are always joy.

We've been to the grocery store, to an upper room, a Buna circle, a Primary classroom, a dinner table. We've seen how Christ is in the ordinary, everyday events of our lives, loving intentionally, doctrinally, and laying down His life for us. We can be filled in our longing to love as He loves.

Just a few days ago, as I was wishing for my Buna circle, needing and wanting a break from my long list of to-dos and my restless children, I prayed. I prayed that someone might remember me. I prayed that I wouldn't have to ask someone to do something and that the Holy Ghost might deliver a message to the right person. As I finished the prayer, I walked outside to see my children talking to our friend Rae. There she was with her big dog and a circle of children, including mine. Just the day before,

Rae had shared with our Relief Society sisters that she wanted to be more available to the Lord. She wanted to set aside her own troubles and be the answer to another sister. As I looked at her and watched her talking to my children, the Spirit whispered to me: *Here's your Buna.*

We sat on the porch and watched kids on scooters. She asked about my day. I said it was exactly as it should be because she was the answer to my prayer. Thanks for being the answer, Rae.

We are "like a mighty army / [we move] the Church of God; [Sisters], we are treading / Where the Saints have trod. / We are not divided; / All one body we: / One in hope and doctrine, / One in charity."[20]

We can love one another as Jesus loves us in ordinary and extraordinary ways. I bear my witness of Jesus Christ as the center of my world. He lives and He loves us, and He needs us to arise and do our part in simple and extraordinary ways. May we all feel the courage to go forward in faith and to do our part, to love one another as He loves us is my prayer.

"A Plea to My Sisters"

To Fill the Measure of Our Creation

Jennifer Reeder

By trade, I am a nineteenth-century historian for the Church. In order to understand early Latter-day Saint women, I look back to the very beginning, when all creatures were commanded to yield fruit in the likeness of their own image (see Genesis 1:21–22, 27–28). Consequently, it was not good for man to be alone—so Eve joined Adam (see Genesis 2:18). Both President Gordon B. Hinckley and President Russell M. Nelson taught that the culminating, crowning act of creation was Woman.[1] After the Fall, Eve and Adam covenanted with God and with each other to overcome mortality and return to the Father, through the mediation of the Lord Jesus Christ. In his first prophetic proclamation, President Nelson admonished us to remember our covenants: "Your commitment to follow the Savior by making covenants with Him and then keeping those covenants will open the door to every spiritual blessing and privilege."[2] The following day, he commented, "To women, I say: whatever your calling, whatever your circumstances, we need your impressions, your insights, and your inspiration. We need your strength!"[3]

President Nelson believes in the mighty capacity of women.

"Step forward!" he said. "Take your rightful and needful place," as Eve did, in the home, the community, and the kingdom of God, as women of strength, conviction, and action.[4] As I have learned about our foremothers, I find myself. Their stories, interwoven with scripture and doctrine taught by prophets of this dispensation, enlarge the purpose of my mortal experience and expand my understanding of my ministry. What is *your* personal mission?[5] What about *your* personal ministry?[6] I invite you to seek the Holy Spirit to testify to you, individually, of how you can step forward.

God commanded Adam and Eve to multiply and replenish the earth, to fill the measure of their creation (see Genesis 1:11, 22, 28; Moses 2:28). What exactly does that mean? My initial reaction was physical procreation—bearing offspring. But with some dictionary research, I understand the definitions differently. To *fill* means to supply or satisfy, to make full, perfect, or complete. *Measure* means the capacity: the whole extent or dimensions, including the length, breadth, and thickness.[7] Scripture teaches us that Christ is the author and finisher of our faith; He creates us—our *measure*—then fills us where we are incomplete (see Hebrews 12:1; Moroni 6:4). Sister Patricia Holland considered a more complete meaning of the measure of our creation: "Every one of us has been designed with a divine role and mission in mind. I believe that if our desires and works are directed to what our heavenly parents have intended for us to be, we will come to feel our part in their plan."[8] These words are intriguing to me: *Divine Role. Mission. Plan. Covenant.*

In December 1832, Joseph Smith described the sanctification of the soul "after it hath filled the measure of its creation" (Doctrine and Covenants 88:19). Previously, he received a revelation for his wife, Emma Smith, which hinted at her divine mission—Doctrine and Covenants 25. In July 1830, shortly after Emma's baptism, the Lord revealed her responsibilities as an elect lady: to comfort and support her husband, to make a collection of hymns, and to expound scripture and exhort the church. The 1828 definitions of those words demonstrate the meaning of this charge. *Expound* means to explain, to lay open the meaning, to clear of obscurity, to interpret. *Exhort* means to encourage, to embolden, to cheer, to advise, to excite, or to give strength, spirit, or courage.[9] The last verse of section 25 tells us that this is the Lord's voice unto all. President Nelson reiterates this charge to women: to step forward, speak out, and fill the measure of our creation.

It was not until 17 March 1842, at the creation of the Nauvoo Relief Society, that Emma assumed her role as Elect Lady or president—one who is elected or chosen.[10] Joseph turned the key to the women, granting them the authority to speak up and speak out.[11] In April 2014, President Dallin H. Oaks encouraged women to recognize the priesthood authority associated with callings as issued by priesthood leaders.[12] President Nelson taught that women are vital associates with the priesthood, that sisters and brothers should walk arm in arm to work together.[13] I love that.

Women engaged in priesthood and doctrine, beginning with Eve and continuing in the Restored Church. The Lord asked Emma to exhort scripture and expound the Church (see Doctrine and Covenants 25:7). President Spencer W. Kimball called for "sister scriptorians."[14] President Boyd K. Packer reaffirmed: "We need women who can teach, women who can speak out."[15] President Nelson said that we can speak with the power and authority of God.[16]

Four women in the early Relief Society learned to speak up

and speak out, and as a result, found their personal missions. Eliza R. Snow was the secretary of the Nauvoo Relief Society. Years later in Salt Lake City, Brigham Young asked her to assist bishops in the organization of ward Relief Societies. The idea of traveling and training overwhelmed her. She wrote that her heart went "pit-a-pat" at the thought of the assignment, but she soon overcame that fear, focusing on her Relief Society mission.[17] She taught women to conquer their apprehensions by seeking holiness through the Holy Ghost. President Nelson said, "We need women who know how to access the power [of] God."[18] That was Eliza. She knew that through her covenants, relationships, and temple work, she filled the measure of her creation.

Initially, Zina Young was "not accustomed to public speaking."[19] Brigham Young called her on a mission to oversee silk manufacture. Zina had a morbid fear of silkworms; a birthmark on her hand resembled a squirmy larva. Nevertheless, she was the first woman in Utah to speak at general conference, calling for a silk association in local Relief Societies.[20] Silk work, along with assisting Eliza R. Snow, gave Zina more confidence and ease.[21] After Eliza's death, Zina served as the third Relief Society General President and conducted the first Relief Society general conference in 1889.[22]

As the president of the Salt Lake City 14th Ward Relief Society, Mary Isabella Horne was so scared to speak that her sisters literally held her.[23] She learned to stand up and extend herself. In 1869, Brigham Young became concerned that so many women were distracted from spiritual things by creating beautiful table settings with elaborate meals and superfluous fashions. He asked Mary Isabella to lead a movement to retrench, or turn back, to basic doctrine and practice.[24] This retrenchment association soon led to the creation of what we know today as the Young Women.

Emmeline B. Wells edited the *Woman's Exponent* from 1877 to 1914. Brigham Young asked her to publish women's biographies and make their words and experiences accessible to other women across the scattered Latter-day Saint settlements.[25] He also gave her a mission to save grain, an early food storage movement.[26] Emmeline said that she was the first person since Joseph of old to be given such a call.[27] She organized a committee and educated women in their local communities on how to store grain.[28]

All of these women learned through their missions and exhortations that they had to act—they had to *do* something. How can you speak up and speak out? How does this help you discover your personal mission and ministry?

I sensed part of my mission in life in 2001 when I first began to pore over the words of the Nauvoo Relief Society minutes. The voices of Emma Smith, Eliza R. Snow, Zina Young, Mary Isabella Horne, and others whispered to me, gently inviting me to enter their world, to discover who they were, what they experienced, and how they embraced their covenants and roles in building the kingdom of God. I yearned to find them, these elect ladies and mothers in Israel, women of this dispensation's Abrahamic covenant. I felt drawn to bring them to light, to make them accessible to women today as part of our shared Latter-day Saint heritage. I needed tools—courses in historiography and research methods, critical analysis, context from women's history, religious history, and nineteenth-century American history, ultimately resulting in a doctoral degree—in order to situate these women. In their stories, I found myself. And I have come to a deeper understanding of the measure of my own creation.

Our "glorious mother Eve" (Doctrine and Covenants 138:39) understood that in order for her to fill the measure of her creation, she had to choose the fruit of the tree of knowledge of good and evil, persuade Adam to partake, and experience the lone and dreary wilderness with its thistles, thorns, and noxious weeds (see Genesis 3:16; Moses 4:22). This charge, indeed, is a conundrum. To fill the measure of our creation, to multiply and replenish, we need to also multiply our sorrows. Eve astutely observed, "Were it not for our transgression we never should have had seed, and never should have known good and evil, and the joy of our redemption, and the eternal life which God giveth unto all the obedient" (Moses 5:11). President Nelson asserted, "We need women who have the courage and vision of our Mother Eve."[29]

I experienced my own lone and dreary wilderness in the middle of graduate school, when I was diagnosed with acute lymphoblastic leukemia in 2010. I gained an imperfect body when I chose to enter mortality. After thirty-five years of abundant health, my DNA slipped and produced abnormal red blood cells. What bad timing—I was right in the middle of developing my personal mission. After two years of treatment, I achieved remission. I finished my dissertation, graduated, landed my dream job at the Church History Department, and moved to Salt Lake City. Six weeks later, in 2013, my leukemia returned. Again, the timing was off. A priesthood blessing reminded me of the measure of my creation. My health would ebb and flow, but the Lord would preserve my life until my work was complete. I endured chemo, radiation, and a bone marrow transplant from my brother Ben. This procedure required the eradication, or death, of my marrow to enable me to receive my new marrow and new life.

While this lone and dreary wilderness nearly killed me, the experience gave my life additional meaning. I learned to fight to fill the measure of my creation. I lived to witness of these women.

I came to understand the need for divine assistance, for Christ to finish my faith and fill me. President Nelson calls upon women to be assertive: "Take your rightful and needful place in your home, in your community, and in the kingdom of God—more than you ever have before."[30] In addition to Eve, Emma, Eliza, Zina, Mary Isabella, and Emmeline, three women from the nineteenth and twentieth centuries demonstrate how we can magnify our capacity, even among thorns and thistles.

Louisa Barnes Pratt took a "rightful place" in her lone and dreary wildernesses; the troubles of life meandered alongside the covenants she made as an early Latter-day Saint. In Nauvoo, her husband, Addison, was called on a mission to Tahiti, leaving her for more than five years with four young daughters. As a single mother, Louisa built a home and supported her family. When the Saints left Nauvoo, Louisa questioned why the leaders who sent her husband to the ends of the earth did not offer her any assistance to move her family. Almon Babbit replied, "They expect you to be smart enough to go yourself without help, and even to assist others." The remark awakened in her a spirit of self-reliance and she asserted that she would show them what she could do. She stood up. In Winter Quarters, Louisa and her daughters lived in a dug-out cave, where she got scurvy and lost her front teeth. She relied on other women for support.[31]

The Pratt family reunited in Salt Lake City. Shortly after his arrival, Addison was called on a second mission to Tahiti; this time Louisa and the girls accompanied him. Their tropical home on Tubuai presented new challenges for Louisa. Her husband traveled often to different islands and, as she had done before, she expanded her personal faith. In August 1851, she caught a cold. She wrote in her journal: "I had a bad night, slept but little;

feel very unwell today; my spirits are drooping and despondent; a thunderstorm awoke me in the night, and for several hours I lay thinking of the storms of life, some of which had fallen on me; and more heavily than even my most familiar friends have been aware of; but hope—soothing, consoling, gladdening hope— sometimes bursts into my often languishing mind and tells me there is a brighter day to come; a day ushered in by the gospel which I so gladly hailed when I heard the sound; 'this hope supported me when I bade my native land farewell.'"[32]

Louisa's sister, Caroline Barnes Crosby, whose family served in the same mission with the Pratts, recounted their arrival: "Our hearts were then full of expectation, whether good or evil we knew not; but we trusted in God and were preserved. And I can truly say that the Lord has been better to us than our fears."[33] Like their fellow members of the Nauvoo Relief Society, Eliza, Zina, and Mary Isabella Horne, Louisa and Caroline overcame discouragement. In the same way they had done in Nauvoo and Winter Quarters, they gathered local women to pray, read the Book of Mormon, and sing Emma Smith's hymns of the Restoration. At first, other missionaries and her daughter translated for her, then little by little, Louisa learned Tahitian, and she truly began to expound scripture—to clear from obscurity and to exhort the people—to embolden, cheer, and uplift. She wrote in her journal on 12 November 1851: "Little do we know what we can do till we make a thorough trial. Past the meridian of life, I learned a new language."[34] She was forty-nine years old. President Nelson said, "Sisters, do you realize the breadth and scope of your influence when you speak those things that come to your heart and mind as directed by the Spirit?"[35]

Louisa Pratt and her family completed their mission and

started for home. However, not having experienced what his wife had with her fellow Latter-day Saint pioneers in a forced exodus across the plains, Addison lost faith and wanted to remain near the coast in California. The definition of "home" forced a wedge in their marriage. Louisa was determined to be with the Saints. She felt "bound with cords of love to the church." Yet her heart broke at the thought of losing her husband as he stayed behind.[36] President Nelson said that "nothing is more crucial to your eternal life than your own conversion."[37] A strong, bedrock, personal conversion will see us across our own wildernesses, Winter Quarters, and hospital rooms.

In 2016, three years after my first bone marrow transplant, my imperfect DNA resurfaced and leukemia recurred. My brother Ben's strong stem cells prevented it from coming into my new marrow, so it went to the next blood barrier: the bone. Leukemic lesions formed on my ribs, spine, and sternum, and I required a second transplant from my other brother, Josh. However, before we could rebuild, I got pneumonia and spent a miserable three months in and out of the hospital as my medical team worked to diagnose a cause and proper treatment. Remember how my priesthood blessing warned me that my health would ebb and flow? Well, I didn't think that would mean coming so close to death multiple times. I was on oxygen for three months and felt all the life and light drain out of me. In my darkest moment, I turned to my community of family, friends, coworkers, and ward members, seeking their focused prayer and faith in my behalf. I felt the presence and ministry of my beloved women. This community became my "host." Their faith lifted me and saved me. It truly was as Lucy Mack Smith stated in the Nauvoo Relief Society, that "we must cherish one another, watch over one another, comfort one another, and gain instruction, that we may all sit down in heaven together."[38] As Sister Marjorie Hinckley has said, "Oh, how we need each other."[39]

Julia Mavimbela provides a beautiful example of President Nelson's charge for women to be engaged in community service, devoted to shepherding God's children. After the violent death of her husband, Julia and her five children left Johannesburg. In the black township of Soweto in apartheid-era South Africa, she reclaimed rocky soil and planted a garden. Local children paid attention to her efforts, and she invited them to assist her, gathering soil, planting seeds, and caring for the plants—basic laws of nature and harvest. With the high cost of water, she instructed them to filter kitchen waste water. She slipped in simple gospel instruction to children drifting through a racially charged and often violent environment with these words: "'Let's all pray. There is someone above us who sees what we are doing. We'll surely see something happen.' At times," she said, "it was as if a telegram or telephone call went directly to the Lord. The next morning I would come to the patch, and there had been a good rain overnight. I can't tell you of the excitement I saw in those beautiful little faces, all convinced that surely there was someone interested in and caring for the work they were doing."[40]

Julia used gardens as schools, instructing her eager students how to read using the words on the seed packets, then extending her literacy efforts to their mothers. She taught the children the words to "I Am a Child of God," and told them to go home and teach their families this simple song with eternal blessings.[41] She followed the counsel Joseph Smith gave to the Nauvoo Relief Society: "Don't be limited in your views with regard to your neighbors' virtues . . . You must enlarge your souls towards others if [you would] do like Jesus, and carry your fellow creatures. . . . As you increase in goodness, let your hearts expand—let them be enlarged towards others."[42]

Julia filled the measure of her creation. She said, "I give thanks to God that He has made me a woman. I give thanks to my creator that He has made me black; that he has fashioned me as I am, with hands, heart, head to serve my people. It can, it should be a glorious thing to be a woman. . . . It is important for women to stand together and rise together to meet our common enemies—illiteracy, poverty, crime, disease, and stupid unjust laws that have made women feel so helpless as to be hopeless."[43] President Nelson taught: "We need women who are devoted to shepherding God's children along the covenant path toward exaltation; women who know how to receive personal revelation; . . . women who know how to call upon the powers of heaven to protect and strengthen children and families; women who teach fearlessly."[44] Julia was fierce.

What is your ministry? It could be in a pile of dirt or teaching children how to read. It could be gathering women to learn and to speak up for their needs and rights. Or teaching someone how to filter clean water from kitchen waste.

In the midst of my first round of leukemia, I served as the ward Relief Society president. I was grateful for the opportunity to serve because it kept me from curling up in a ball and staying in bed all day. I made phone calls and sent text messages and emails from my bed, or had people come visit me instead of me visiting them. It was an incredible experience and gave me a reason to live. During my second transplant, I was able to work from home. I would be rolled up in a ball on the couch, unable to talk due to coughing, but I would pull out my laptop and get into the lives of these women to find a spark of life in myself. I came alive. Their lives expanded my world of pneumonia and leukemia into a much larger one—in fact, the kingdom of God.

Carol Gray is an example of a woman who envisioned the kingdom. She reflected Joseph Smith's words to the Nauvoo Relief Society: "Ye are now placed in a situation where you can act according to those sympathies which God has planted in your bosoms. If you live up to these principles how great and glorious!—if you live up to your privilege, the angels cannot be restrained from being your associates."[45] Like Julia Mavimbela, Carol saw a need and utilized her local resources in Sheffield, England, to minister to those in extreme need. Her patriarchal blessing told her that she would be saved for a specific purpose. She miraculously survived a terminal cancer diagnosis at the age of twenty-eight. Years later she watched news coverage of the Balkan wars with footage of people in Serbian refugee camps. Carol felt a call to do something beyond sending money to a charitable organization.[46]

President Packer encouraged women to combine their mighty forces for good: "We need women who are organized and women who can organize. We need women with executive ability who can plan and direct and administer; women who can teach, women who can speak out."[47] Carol did just that; she solicited donations from her ward and stake to send to the Bosnian warzone. Local news venues picked up her story, and after three weeks, she had thirty-eight tons of aid overflowing her church building. She made arrangements for a charitable organization to deliver the contributions to Serbia, but two days before the designated charity was to leave, they ran out of funds and cancelled the trip. Carol couldn't find another group to transport the materials for her, but she did come upon a convoy that was willing to have her join them. She secured a large truck, and because she was already uninsurable due to her preexisting cancer condition, going into a war zone didn't have the same ramifications it may have had for other people. This was her "bonus time." Carol drove past shellfire, minefields, and mass graves to minister to people in extreme need. She returned home knowing God had "gotten her into something that she couldn't turn away from."[48] President Nelson said, "My dear sisters, whatever your calling, whatever your circumstances, we need your impressions, your insights, and your inspiration. . . . You sisters possess distinctive capabilities and special intuition you have received as gifts from God."[49]

Carol eventually participated in twenty-three convoys, spending a large amount of money to deliver materials to locations even the United Nations couldn't enter. She said, "I'm not a brave woman. I'm not a Mother Teresa, nor a Joan of Arc, so please don't go thinking anything like that. I'm just an ordinary housewife from England who got involved in something that has escalated, and I just have to go along with it."[50]

As sisters in Zion, we have a long and deep heritage—from our glorious Mother Eve to the women of this dispensation—Emma Smith, Louisa Barnes Pratt, Julia Mavimbela, and Carol Gray. They teach me about my divine mission and how to fill the measure of my creation within my circumstances and resources. Each of us encounters setbacks and stumbling blocks; we can choose whether we sit down and stand by, or stand up and take action. Joseph Smith, President Nelson, and our Heavenly Father have all invited us to stand up, to speak up, speak out, and contribute to our homes, communities, and the kingdom of God. President Nelson bestowed an apostolic blessing on women, including *me*, including *you*: "I . . . bless you to rise to your full stature, to fulfill the measure of your creation, as we walk arm in arm in this sacred work."[51] Jesus Christ is the author and finisher of our faith—our Creator and our Savior who fills us. We have the incredible opportunity to partner with Him.

CHOOSING PERSONAL RESPONSIBILITY AND ACCOUNTABILITY

Lauren A. Barnes

Choosing, or agency, is "the privilege of choice which was introduced by God the Eternal Father to all his spirit children in the premortal state."[1] This was a great gift or privilege we selected in the premortal existence. Because we chose to come to earth and follow Christ's plan, we are able to be agents to "act . . . and not to be acted upon" (2 Nephi 2:26) and to be "free to act for [ourselves]" (2 Nephi 10:23). We know that each of us has the power and ability to choose—and that power is a privilege.

"*Responsibility* is to recognize ourselves as being the cause for the effects or results of our choices—good or bad."[2] Once we make a choice, we recognize that we are responsible for the choice and the effects or consequences of that choice. We "will be punished for [our] own sins" (Articles of Faith 1:2).

Accountability is "the quality or state of being accountable; *esp.*: an obligation or willingness to accept responsibility or to account for one's actions."[3] Thus, we realize that one can be responsible without accountability. However, it is best when we take accountability for our choices. Accountants in the financial world are responsible for making sure things measure up and play out as they should. If we apply this same principle to our own lives, taking accountability allows us to have more integrity regarding our choices and live more fully. It can be hard to be accountable if we don't feel like we need to be accountable to somebody else. In Doctrine and Covenants 42:32 we read, "Every man shall be made accountable unto me." We are responsible for the choices we make, and we are accountable to our Heavenly Father for how we use our agency. I invite you to think about how you can make accountability more personal.

Elder Lynn G. Robbins gave a talk at BYU Education Week entitled, "Be 100 Percent Responsible." He states, "Assuming responsibility and being accountable for our choices are agency's complementary principles."[4] This means that when used in conjunction with each other, choosing responsibility and being accountable for our choices enhances our ability to feel integrity and be more at peace with our Father in Heaven.

THE GIFT OF AGENCY

In the beginning, God placed Adam and Eve in the garden and gave them choices. Eventually, Eve, in her wisdom, partook of the fruit. She made a choice that has blessed us and allows for our growth and learning as Heavenly Father's children. As moral beings, we are agents unto ourselves. We are free to choose. Doctrine and Covenants 101:78 states, "Every man may act in doctrine and principle . . . according to the *moral agency* which I have given unto him, that every man may be accountable for his own sins in the day of judgment" (emphasis added). We are not only accountable for our sins, but we are also accountable for all the good we do. We must choose how we want to personally affect and influence those around us and how we want to grow individually.

Elder D. Todd Christofferson suggests three basic elements of moral agency: "First, there must be alternatives among which to choose. . . . Second, for us to have agency, we must not only have alternatives, but we must also know what they are. . . . Third is the next element of agency: the freedom to make choices."[5] We know from scripture that alternatives exist and that there is opposition in all things (see 2 Nephi 2:11); there are "both things to act and things to be acted upon" (2 Nephi 2:14). We are those who act—or, in other words, make choices. We utilize the gospel light we are given, and we're able to better use and exercise agency. We are blessed to be in a land which allows us the opportunity to choose and the freedom and opportunity to exercise our agency.

President Dallin H. Oaks has a powerful presence and a way with words. Whenever he gets up to speak, I know he will usually say something bold. In 1999, almost twenty years ago, he stated, "We are responsible to use our agency in a world of choices. It will not do to pretend that our agency has been taken away when we are not free to exercise it without unwelcome consequences."[6] We need to recognize that we always have agency; we are not forced to make decisions, and we should not act like we have no ability to choose when we don't like the consequences of a choice. We always have a choice. We always have agency.

Many of us are mothers. I don't pretend to have all the answers and realize most of you could teach me about parenting—I only have two kids and they're both younger than seven. In looking to our Heavenly Father's example, we see that as a perfect parent He never forced His children. He allowed us to choose to come to earth in the premortal world and continues to allow us to choose in our daily life. Yes, there are consequences. Yes, He knows what they are. Yes, He experiences pain and suffering and sadness as a result of some of our choices. But He loves us and wants us all to be happy and experience joy. However, He never forces His children. Likewise, we cannot force our children—or anybody else. We must allow our children to test and use their agency just as we learn from our Heavenly Father. We are only *responsible* for what we can control and what is within the bounds of our own agency. I know that it can be hard to allow our children to use their agency and learn about accountability and responsibility—especially with teenagers or even toddlers or even adult children. A wise colleague of mine refers to something called "escape velocity"; and I apologize if the physics of this is completely off—he states that teenagers must have enough friction in order to take off. We need to allow our children to struggle a bit with their agency and learn for themselves. Only by doing this do we allow them to grow and properly exercise agency.

RESPONSIBILITY

When I think of the word *responsibility*, I tend to think of my many responsibili*ties*. My guess is most of you do the same. I'll bet you could quickly and easily come up with at least three things you need to do today. However, personal responsibility is different from our many responsibilities. When I looked up "responsibility" in the LDS Topical Guide, it says, "See also Accountability; Dependability; Duty; Leadership; Marriage, Fatherhood; Marriage, Motherhood; Steadfastness; Stewardship."[7] There are many things we have responsibility over or that responsibility is related to. Personal responsibility means that we are responsible for our own personal wellbeing and development. Instead of thinking of the many responsibilities we have, we need to focus on our own personal growth, well-being, and development. We're responsible for ourselves.

Elder Lynn G. Robbins wisely stated, "One of Satan's most crafty strategies to gain control of our agency isn't a frontal attack on our agency but a sneaky backdoor assault on responsibility."[8] Satan is so creative and sneaky. We can see many of his backdoor attacks in recent days; for example, freedom of speech being twisted to support, create, and protect pornography. In recent years, we've seen an increase in reports of sexual assault without responsibility on the part of the perpetrator and outright victim blaming. With an increase in so many problems, issues, struggles, and difficulties in the world, we need to be aware of our responsibility and the ways the culture around us may twist responsibility in a way that dulls our sensitivity to the Spirit.

Elder Robbins goes on to say, "If Satan is not successful in fully separating agency from responsibility, one of his backup schemes is to dull or minimize feelings of responsibility."[9] If Satan can't convince us that we have no responsibility, he can at least trick us into thinking it's not *completely* our fault. I want you to imagine that you're at a party and they're serving red Kool-Aid. It just so happens that they also have white carpet. You have to be really careful. At one point you go off into a corner to maybe check your phone, you set your drink down, and then accidentally knock it over, spilling the red Kool-Aid all over the host's beautiful white carpet. Where does your mind go first? Nobody saw you. Does it really matter? How responsible are you for that stain?

Elder Robbins suggests a list of nineteen items he has called "The Anti-Responsibility List":

1. Blaming others. . . .
2. Rationalizing or justifying. . . .
3. Making excuses. . . .
4. Minimalizing or trivializing sin. . . .
5. Hiding. . . .
6. Covering up. . . .
7. Fleeing from responsibility. . . .
8. Abandoning responsibility. . . .
9. Denying or lying. . . .
10. Rebelling. . . .
11. Complaining and murmuring. . . .
12. Finding fault and getting angry. . . .
13. Making demands and entitlements. . . .
14. Doubting, losing hope, giving up, and quitting. . . .
15. Indulging in self-pity and a victim mentality. . . .
16. Being indecisive or being in a spiritual stupor. . . .
17. Procrastinating. . . .
18. Allowing fear to rule. . . .
19. Enabling.[10]

Looking at this list, what stands out to you? Most of us probably have our favorites and our go-tos from this list that we use to shirk responsibility. For me, I can easily blame others, rationalize, and indulge in self-pity. I'm really, really good at those. In fact, if I had spilled the Kool-Aid and stained the host's carpet, my honest first thought would be, "What kind of person has white carpet and serves a colored drink? This is totally their fault!" Trust me—we had light-colored carpet in our first townhouse rental with a toddler who was potty training; I'm very good at blaming other people.

What gets in the way of responsibility for you? Alma 42:30 states: "Do not endeavor to excuse yourself in the least point." That's a pretty bold statement; we can't endeavor to excuse ourselves in the least point. For me, and probably for many others, some of the main culprits and things that get in the way of our taking personal responsibility include pride, fear, anger, and a desire for justice. As a quick note, it's important to recognize and distinguish between shame and guilt in regards to personal responsibility. Shame leads us to think *I am a bad person*, whereas guilt will have us think, *I did something bad*. Shame is never healthy. We are not bad people; we are children of God. Guilt, however, can be healthy and motivate us to change. We see that in the scriptures with Alma the Younger where he was racked with guilt to the point that he had no more desire to do bad once his mind turned to Christ's Atonement (see Alma 36). Guilt is okay and even healthy. We have the light of Christ and agency and are given the ability to feel positively or negatively in our reactions to our choices and their consequences.

If we're going back to the anti-responsibility list and looking at some of the common ways people avoid responsibility, it may seem difficult to determine the difference between when somebody is merely explaining or when they're making an excuse for their behavior. Successful people will "repent, get back on their feet, and continue moving forward in faith."[11] They may give an explanation or a reason for the lack of success, but not an excuse. An explanation allows one to give the backstory or update the other person on what happened and how they got there. An excuse is usually a defense, justification, or an alibi. So even if I'm right to say that having white carpet and serving red Kool-Aid is dumb, saying so offers a justification, not an explanation, and doesn't do me any good in the long run.

"Going to the anti-responsibility list is counterproductive, *even if you are right*."[12] This can be a helpful tip for all of us in relationships. How many times could we choose the relationship instead of being right? Choose personal responsibility and don't give excuses or use the anti-responsibility list. We need to choose humility, healthy relationships, and connection over personal pride, fear, anger, and whatever else gets in the way of us choosing responsibility. As a therapist, I feel I must make a note here: Nobody should ever be in an emotionally, financially, physically, or sexually abusive relationship. That is not a time to choose humility; that is a time to choose boundaries and personal safety and health. By choosing humility, I'm not saying you should enable, live in fear, indulge in self-pity, or do anything else from the anti-responsibility list. There is a fine line, but we can choose humility and choose healthy relationships over excuses, and this allows us to choose accountability.

ACCOUNTABILITY

Because of our agency and ability to choose, we are responsible for the choices we make. Accountability is an obligation or willingness to accept responsibility or to account for one's actions. We know that each of us with the mental and emotional capacity for accountability will be held accountable to our Heavenly Father in the last days.

We can teach accountability to our children and others around us. The best way to do this, of course, is teaching by example. Think back to the Kool-Aid example. What was your honest first thought after realizing you'd spilled it? Was it to go tell the host, take responsibility, and be accountable for your actions? Or was it to use a method from the anti-responsibility list? We must not let pride get in the way. We're going to mess up. We're not perfect. Only one person on the earth ever was. We need to accept our imperfections and keep trying. I mess up regularly with my children. In fact, sometimes it is my responsibility to apologize to my children. I end up doing this multiple times every week. Apologizing when we make mistakes helps our children know that we're not perfect (which I'm sure they'll remind us of in their teenage years and beyond). But more important, it shows them that we're not perfect, and we don't expect *them* to be. It teaches them the value of continually trying and striving for growth and learning. We're on this earth to learn, grow, and form meaningful, deep relationships.

One of the things most parents will teach their children is the importance of saying "I'm sorry." This introduces the concepts of agency and responsibility. It allows our children to reflect upon the choices they made and take responsibility for actions that may have hurt another. We can introduce the concept of accountability but encourage our children (and ourselves) to add to this, "What can I do to help?" By introducing this question after stating, "I'm sorry," we can take accountability and learn how to make amends.

In his book *Man's Search for Meaning*, Viktor Frankl describes his situation in a concentration camp. Everything was taken from him and the other prisoners there. They were in pain and agony, unsure of how long they would live and unsure of whether they'd see their family or friends ever again. One of his greatest statements is, "Everything can be taken from a man but one thing: *the last of the human freedoms—to choose one's attitude in any given set of circumstances, to choose one's own way.*"[13] Accept yourself as the person in control of your own life. There are always things we can control. You may not have a choice about your circumstances or your environment, but you *always* have a choice in how you react and how you choose to exercise your agency.

We are accountable to our Savior and Heavenly Father. This means we must strive to develop a personal relationship directly with Them. How do you believe Heavenly Father sees you? What do you believe about the Savior's Atonement? Does it include you? Does He really know you and your struggles? Some hypothesize that our relationship with our earthy parents, and particularly our father, may mirror our relationship with our Heavenly Father. That may be a good place to look and start dissecting how you feel about your Heavenly Father and how you believe He views you. Build your testimony. I believe it is vital for each person to struggle a bit with doctrine. This could be a big or small struggle, filled with simple or complex emotions. Only through struggle and questioning can we grow and develop a strong personal testimony. We must seek answers to our questions about the gospel.

Responsibility and accountability are *personal*. This means that they "[relate] to, or [affect] a particular person."[14] I'm going to share a little bit about my personal background and history— not because I think it will apply to you directly—but because it's important to realize that each of us has *personal* responsibility and accountability for our personal use of agency.

In 2003, my dad was in a brutal car accident; he ended up flipping the car multiple times and was scalped by the glass window, resulting in chronic pain and permanent disabilities. After this accident, my mother, who had been the primary home-maker (and was really quite good at it) was suddenly forced into the reality of becoming the primary breadwinner for our family. Luckily, she had a bachelor's degree. We sold our house and lived with friends in Utah for a little while. Much of my parents' savings, disability insurance, and retirement went to paying for medical expenses and helping us survive for the months we were without my dad's income while Mom looked for work and cared for my dad. During that time, I learned the importance of food storage, savings, education, and hard work.

In 2004, President Hinckley gave a talk in which he encouraged women to "get all of the education that you possibly can."[15] His message was reiterated over the next year and continued echoing in my ears; I felt like he was talking to me. I knew I would need to get a good education. My brother's friend Aaron came and dropped my brother and me off at Brigham Young University in the fall of 2005. After we arrived in Provo, Aaron and I ended up talking into the wee hours of the night and really hit it off. One month later, Aaron moved to Provo as well, with $1,000 to his name. He found a job, and we started hanging out and dating. He proposed on my eighteenth birthday in the middle of my freshman year at BYU, and we were married in August 2006.

We knew we'd want to start a family, but didn't know when the time would be right, so I dedicated myself to school so I could graduate as fast as possible; I often took eighteen credit hours while working part-time and being involved in research with faculty. I graduated with my bachelor's degree and applied for BYU's Marriage and Family Therapy master's program. When I still wasn't pregnant toward the end of the master's program, Aaron and I decided that I should apply for the PhD program and just see what happened. I really love school and learning and it was really scary for me to think about getting a job at that point. I applied for the PhD program in December 2009. Weeks later, we found out we were pregnant—and due the day the MFT PhD program would start. By divine intervention, I was also admitted to the PhD program.

I remember thinking, *Is this one of those tests where I'm supposed to choose the better option? What is the better option? Is it selfish of me to want an education* and *a family? Is that even possible? Should I support Aaron in completing his education and stop mine to stay home?* After a lot of prayer, conversations, and tears, we decided I would pursue the PhD program and we'd try to balance life with a family and school.

It was hard right from the beginning. Our son ended up being delivered through an emergency C-section and was in the NICU for the first few weeks of his life. In addition, I had pretty severe postpartum depression and anxiety. There were moments I saw things crawling on the walls that weren't there and moments I felt like going to a hotel away from the baby's crying so I could just sleep for more than forty-five minutes. I felt so much resentment toward Aaron because he wasn't the one breastfeeding. I was sleep-deprived and often miserable.

I wondered if I was being punished for getting an education and whether I'd made a bad decision in beginning the PhD program. But I also feel like my education saved me. Because of my studies, I had great friends and colleagues who gave me support I wouldn't have had if I were home full-time. I was able to use research skills to the benefit of our family. I challenged myself and learned to be a better student. I had great mentors and managed to get through. It was my responsibility to follow through with the choices I'd made.

A couple of years later, I was working at Center for Change

and we had our daughter. As I was in the hospital bed getting prepped for an epidural for yet another C-section, I received an email asking me to apply for the clinical director position in the Marriage and Family Therapy program at BYU. I chuckled out loud while talking to Aaron, thinking there was no way I'd apply or take a faculty position. From what I'd seen, faculty always seemed worn out and tired.

After our daughter's birth, I took a few weeks off, but the hormones and work of "balancing" life and kids was absolutely insane. I got a bit stir-crazy at home. I couldn't seem to find joy. I always felt like I fell short. After some persuading, I applied for the position.

Fast forward a few months—I was offered the BYU faculty position as clinical director. I started full time in October 2013. This job has been such a blessing to us. It's allowed me great flexibility and pushes me to grow in ways I couldn't imagine. I still have my moments of despair, doubt, depression, anxiety, perfectionism, and wanting to give up, but I have also felt great love, joy, support, and closeness.

In the past year, my dad's chronic pain and mental decline turned into fairly severe emotional and even physical abuse. I've watched my parents' marriage of thirty-eight years come to an end. My dad's mental illness took over to a point that he is now limited in his clarity and ability to exercise his agency. My mom is a beacon of strength and such a great example of womanhood and commitment to her religious covenants. I admire her courage, love, determination, commitment, work ethic, and femininity. My dad is now remarried and living in Cuba with support and love from a new family. I still love him as my father and hope he will find healing and peace. But I also believe in the importance of boundaries for personal and family health.

I have the ability to choose. There is *always* the opportunity to choose. If nothing else, we can choose and strive for happiness and choose how we will feel.

I am responsible for my choices. I ultimately chose to write all those papers, go to school even though it was hard, and write my dissertation—mostly one-handed while breastfeeding. It may be hard, but it is my responsibility to follow through with my choices.

I ultimately chose to pursue a PhD, a faculty career, and have children. Because of those choices, we have made and continue to make many sacrifices (especially on Aaron's part). The LDS Proclamation to the World states, "Fathers and mothers are obligated to help one another as equal partners."[16] We are each accountable for our choices. As a couple we need to work together to achieve our goals and be helpmeets (e.g., *ezer kenegdo*).[17]

We need to trust that each individual can figure out his or her own purpose. Why is it so hard when people get a different answer than ourselves? It is *personal* responsibility and accountability. We need to lift those around us and support other women in their personal choices. We need to remember we are only accountable for our own.

I invite you sisters to choose responsibility and accountability and remember not to go to the anti-responsibility list—even if you are right. I invite you to choose to love one another, minister to each other, connect with others, and form lasting relationships. I realize this can be hard when those closest to us are hurting or making choices we don't agree with. However, again, we must remember it is *personal* responsibility and accountability. We should and can choose to love others as commanded. God will help us if we allow Him. He wants us to be connected to each other.

"The more we are like Jesus Christ, the less likely we are to judge unrighteously, to give up on someone, or to quit a worthy cause. Even though we may sometimes give up on ourselves, *the Savior never gives up on us,* because He is perfect in His long-suffering: 'Notwithstanding their sins, my bowels are filled with compassion towards them' (D&C 101:9)."[18]

I know that our Savior lives and has a perfect love and hope for each of us. He and our Heavenly Father can help us work toward choosing personal responsibility and accountability and help us utilize the necessary skills in our families. We can choose to be humble, minister to others, connect and form relationships, and we can choose to love and express charity toward those around us. I know as we do these things and follow the Savior, we will be blessed.

Up, Awake,
Ye Defenders of Zion

Joy D. Jones

I love visiting with sisters throughout the Church. I can honestly say that, wherever I go, I meet unwavering women who are willing to stand for truth and righteousness. They shine—as do you today. The sisters I meet tell me stories of their challenges and trials. Yet these wonderful daughters of God continue to "press forward with a steadfastness in Christ" (2 Nephi 31:20).

It may be that in our daily lives, some of us are seldom asked to stand—literally or figuratively—to defend the gospel of Jesus Christ and His kingdom here on earth. On the other hand, some of us may be required to speak up on a regular basis to defend truth: perhaps at school, at work, with friends, or even with family. Sisters, I promise you that whether it's in the boardroom or the bakery, at some point, as a disciple of Christ, you will be called upon to articulate what you know and believe. How much easier it will be if you are prepared.

So how do we react when a situation presents itself to speak up for Jesus Christ and His Church, to which we belong? Let's consider several possibilities:

We've all heard of the proverbial deer in the headlights. Has this ever been you? Do we freeze? Do we struggle to know what to say or do? This choice has its consequences—especially for the deer!

Here is another choice—run! Avoid confrontation at all cost! Don't get involved. Don't let others know what you really believe. This has its consequences also—one of the biggest being missed opportunity and regret, not only for ourselves, but also for those who might have benefited from our words.

Let's consider our third alternative—to stand as a witness. As President M. Russell Ballard stated: "When we covenant in the waters of baptism to 'stand as witnesses of God at all times and in all things, and in all places,' we're not talking solely about fast and testimony meetings. It may not always be easy, convenient, or politically correct to stand for truth and right, but it is always the right thing to do. Always."[1]

Let me give you an example a young mother shared with me:

"Occasionally I go out with a few friends for an evening when we visit together, get a change of pace from our daily routines, and strengthen one another. My friends are all active, calling-holding sisters in the gospel. We have gone through ups and downs of having babies and trying to figure out motherhood together.

"One particular night we decided to go to dinner and enjoy a nice relaxing evening away from our normal responsibilities. It was heavenly! But soon after we were served our dinners, two of my friends started talking negatively about our bishop. They did not agree with something the bishop had said in ward council and complained about how it affected them in their callings. This quickly led to a discussion about certain aspects of the gospel and eventually to more murmuring about sacred things.

"I sat in disbelief as I listened to these valiant women I love slide down a slippery slope of grumbling and protesting. I was very uncomfortable and knew that one of us needed to say something before it got any worse. I also knew that my friends would not be thrilled with my contradicting what they were saying or disagreeing with their complaints. I was nervous to the point of shaking. I felt sick to my stomach with the idea of not saying anything but also felt sick at the idea of being the one friend in the group who called everyone out on what they were saying. That just isn't the cool thing to do when you are out on a girls' night! But my conscience eventually won out.

"I spoke up and expressed my feelings. I also shared how difficult it must be for our bishop to have to come to ward council and say hard things that he likely knew would not be agreed with. I jokingly said how grateful I was that I would never be a bishop and that I was grateful that our current bishop was willing to take on such responsibility.

"I tried to finish my words on a light note, but I was still met with a few moments of awkward silence. I had gone against the grain of what was being said, and my opinion was not exactly the popular vote. Thankfully we were able to move on to another topic without too much discomfort. The funny thing is that the next day one of my friends, who was sitting at the table with me the previous night but hadn't said anything, stopped by my house to thank me for speaking up the night before. She felt remorse and didn't like what had been expressed but didn't know how to change the subject.

"I can honestly say that I came home from that girls' night feeling happy that I had spoken up. I was scared and nervous to do it, but speaking up strengthened my testimony of what I was saying and helped me feel more confident in my relationship with my Heavenly Father."[2]

Joseph Smith wasn't at a girls' night on one of the many noted occasions when he had to stand up for his beliefs. He was in jail in Missouri. And that setting required a strong reaction. You know the story: The guards who held him boasted of the atrocities they had committed among the Latter-day Saints. Finally, Joseph could stand it no longer and stood, as majesty in chains, proclaiming: "SILENCE, ye fiends of the infernal pit! In the name of Jesus Christ I rebuke you, and command you to be still; I will not live another minute and bear such language. Cease such talk, or you or I die THIS INSTANT!"[3]

Now, we probably won't use exactly these words in our standing up, but we can follow the Prophet's example even as we paraphrase just a little—and, in most situations, quite a lot.

Sometimes compromise represents a far greater risk than courage. As difficult as it is to stand for truth, it is much harder to live with the consequences of moral failure.

About 500 years ago, Martin Luther was faced with the choice between capitulation or excommunication. He then spoke the words that began the great Reformation: "My conscience is captive to the Word of God," he said. "I cannot and I will not recant anything, for to go against conscience is neither right nor safe. . . . Here I stand, I cannot do otherwise."[4]

These examples are extreme but instructive. Elder Robert D. Hales said, "We can pray for guidance about when to speak, what to say, and yes, on some occasions, when to be still. Remember, our children and family members [and all those around us] already chose to follow the Savior in their premortal realm.

Sometimes it is only by their own life's experiences that those sacred feelings are awakened again."[5]

I love this example from the *New Era*. Heather from Virginia tells about her high school English class, where the teacher asked the class to express their opinions about relevant but controversial issues. The teacher would read a statement and if you supported it, you were to move to the left side of the room. If you didn't, you were to move to the right of the room. The first statement that the teacher read was "'coed sleepovers should be allowed.' . . . There was a brief pause, then a giddy stampede to the left side of the room. [She] was the only one left sitting.

"In [her] mind it wasn't an option to go to the left side of the room. [She] knew what [she] believed. So [she] stood up, faced [her] friends, and told them [she] didn't think coed sleepovers were appropriate."

Heather faced some difficulty for standing up for her beliefs, but she says that after class, "a girl from my class stopped me in the hall. 'I just wanted to say that was really brave of you,' she said. 'I don't think I would be able to do that.'"

Heather said that even though that experience was a hard thing to do, it helped her to define herself. Because of the influence of the gospel in her life, she knew what side of the line she stood on and knew that nothing could change that. She felt that she was a much happier person because she knew that the Lord would be with her when she stood up for her beliefs.[6]

Sister Bonnie Oscarson, speaking in general conference, said, "The Lord needs us to be brave, steadfast, and immovable warriors who will defend His plan and teach the upcoming generations His truths."[7]

Are we who are disciples of Christ willing to follow Sister

Oscarson's counsel even when we risk a loss of respect? Are we willing to face opposing opinions without being oppositional? Are we willing to step off the sidelines when it comes to defending the truth—and still not be defensive?

It might help to remember the wisdom of Elder Jeffrey R. Holland: "You will one day find yourself called upon to defend your faith or perhaps even endure some personal abuse simply because you are a member of The Church of Jesus Christ of Latter-day Saints. Such moments will require both courage and courtesy on your part."[8]

Sisters, our foremothers showed us the way, demonstrating both the courage and courtesy Elder Holland is encouraging for us: "In February 1870 the territorial government of Utah granted women the right to vote in government elections. At that time, the territory of Wyoming was the only other place in the United States where women were given this right. Later the national government rescinded this privilege as part of the punishment for Latter-day Saints living the law of plural marriage. But Latter-day Saint women remained vocal and articulate about their rights. Many sisters actively sought women's suffrage, or the right to vote. Their increasing ability to speak articulately was a blessing when they needed to represent themselves as strong, dignified, and ennobled women. Through their efforts, they regained the right to vote when Utah was granted statehood in the United States of America. They also gained the respect of other women's movements in the United States and around the world."[9]

Some of our most articulate moments and greatest influence come with how we live, by being happy in a family, happy in being obedient, happy in the way we dress, serve, and work. It sometimes seems increasingly in vogue to joke in demeaning ways about children, husbands, prophets, service in the kingdom, etc., which may provide another opportunity for each of us to speak up.

Did everyone agree with the Savior as He taught His seemingly new doctrine to the Jews? Of course not. Did He tolerate the sins of His day that we see so rampant before us today? No, He did not stay silent. He was bold in His proclamations because He knew He was doing His Father's will. Not everyone agreed with what He taught, but He stood for the truth. He had enemies, but He loved them and always treated others with kindness. His example stands supreme.

There is, as the Savior demonstrated, a powerful difference between showing sincere love to someone versus tolerating what a person is doing. We can still love another person and not support his or her choices. As Elder Holland said, we can show courtesy and respect while still addressing issues of disagreement. And we must make appropriate judgments to protect ourselves and our families. As Alma taught, we can be bold but not overbearing (see Alma 38:12).

We all remember the story of Esther from the Old Testament. Her country of Persia was similar to today's culture in that life was driven by pleasure, possessions, and power. Esther was queen when Haman, the king's minister, plotted the destruction of all the Jews. She had the opportunity to be silent or to go before her husband-king—which was forbidden—risking possible death to save her fellow Jews. How courageous were her words as she made the decision to go forward with her plan, saying, "If I perish, I perish" (Esther 4:16). Her life was on the line. Ultimately, though, Esther's plea for her people stopped Haman's plots, and the Jews were saved.

In those five simple words is a lifetime of preparation. A lifetime of commitment. A lifetime of faith and courage. "If I perish, I perish." She put her full trust in the Lord.

Do we trust the Lord as we open our mouths? Our words have power to influence for good. I believe the Lord has chosen us as modern-day Esthers, dear sisters, to come to earth at this most critical time, "for such a time as this" (Esther 4:14). We can, one by one, stand for truth, stand for righteousness, stand for goodness and decency.

Do you remember when Alma went into the land of the Zoramites? These were former members of the Church of God who had become dissenters. Rather than taking up weapons to fight against these dissenters, Alma realized that "as the preaching of the word had a great tendency to lead the people to do that which was just—yea, it had had more powerful effect upon the minds of the people than the sword, or anything else, which had happened unto them—therefore Alma thought it was expedient that they should try the virtue of the word of God" (Alma 31:5).

Note that the *words* they spoke were more powerful than any other weapon they could use. That is the power of the word of God. As sisters in Zion, we can, at the right time and in the right place, allow the Spirit of God to help us when we are called upon to defend the truth. There is nothing more powerful than the truth. When the Savior spoke up to those around Him, He insightfully taught us, "I am the way, the truth, and the life" (John 14:6). We must never underestimate His power to change and lift and inspire lives.

Recently, Sister Sharon Eubank taught: "Each of us needs to be better at articulating the reasons for our faith. How do you feel about Jesus Christ? Why do you stay in the Church? Why do you believe the Book of Mormon is scripture? Where do you get your peace? Why does it matter that the prophet has something to say [today]? How do you know he is a real prophet? Use your voice and your power to articulate what you know and feel— on social media, in quiet conversations with your friends, when you're chatting with your grandchildren. Tell them why you believe, what it feels like, if you ever doubted, how you got through it, and what Jesus Christ means to you. As the Apostle Peter said, 'Be not afraid . . . ; but sanctify the Lord God in your hearts: and be ready always to give an answer to every man that asketh you a reason of the hope that is in you' (1 Peter 3:14–15)."[10]

Sisters, may we all rise up and be covenant disciples of Jesus Christ. May we proclaim through word and deed, as did Mormon: "Behold, I am a disciple of Jesus Christ, the Son of God. I have been called of him to declare his word among his people, that they might have everlasting life" (3 Nephi 5:13).

"That We May All Sit Down in Heaven Together"

Sharon Eubank and Reyna I. Aburto

Sister Eubank: The theme of this year's Brigham Young University Women's Conference is "Strengthen One Another in the Lord." What a perfect definition of true ministering! The focus for our presentation this afternoon comes from a statement by Lucy Mack Smith, the mother of the Prophet Joseph Smith. She said, "We must cherish one another, watch over one another, comfort one another and gain instruction, that we may all sit down in heaven together."[1] Sister Aburto and I love the idea that after we serve each other and learn together, we can all be united in heaven. To me, that sounds like paradise—sitting down and enjoying the relationships of all those I loved on this earth.

We want to share a portion of President Russell M. Nelson's address at the General Authority training that occurred just before the April 2018 general conference. He had just spent the majority of his talk explaining the new ministering program, and this is how he closed his remarks:

"As we embrace this newer, higher, and holier way to minister, doors will open, and people will be blessed. Hearts will be healed, and burdens lifted. The doctrine of Christ will be taught and testimonies of Him will be strengthened. Lives will be saved, and joy will be felt in all homes of the Latter-day Saints."[2]

A higher and holier way to minister. We feel Lucy Mack Smith had the vision from the very beginning: cherishing, watching over, comforting, and learning from one another, we will be doing the higher and holier ministering that our prophet has asked us to do.

Sister Aburto is now going to share about learning to *cherish* one another.

Sister Aburto: A few years ago, my two youngest children left on missions at about the same time. It was hard for me and my husband to adapt to our new life without our children. We had to redefine our daily routines, and reinvent the way we grocery shopped, cooked, and entertained ourselves.

It was during that period of adjustment that I received a new companion for visiting teaching. When I saw her name, I thought: "This is going to be interesting!"

If you look at us, it may look like we don't have much in common. At that time, she was a newlywed, she is very young, and she is very blonde!

Nevertheless, we started visiting the sisters that were assigned to us. Even though she had two jobs and attended school full-time, she made our visits a priority and we were always able to work around her schedule and minister to our sisters.

It didn't take us long to realize that we had a lot in common. For example, she had served a Spanish-speaking mission in California and she loved Mexican food. For a few months we would meet at my house with one of the sisters we visited, and we would cook different Mexican dishes.

This wonderful sister filled the void that my daughter had left, and we have become best friends; we are now "besties" or

"BFFs." From her, I have learned about resilience and faith and how to live the gospel more joyfully.

Sometimes we may feel that we don't have anything in common. Occasionally, I hear women say, "They assigned me to someone I have nothing in common with, so it will not work out." I want to recommend that the higher, holier way of ministering is to make us feel comfortable sitting down with each other, even if we think we are very different. We can sometimes be hard on each other as women; we might start judging, comparing, and competing, rather than having compassion and charity. But we can change that culture in the Church, and we must.

It truly doesn't matter who has ten kids and who has one, who is a scientist and who has a third-grade education, or who wears pants and who wears a skirt. To those who say we don't have anything in common, I would suggest that those superficial things matter the least. What unites us is our divine heritage, the people who help us grow spiritually, the assignments we receive from the Lord, our faith in God's plan, our love of Jesus Christ, and our sisterhood in Heavenly Father's family.

I know the theme of this session is inspired because it is the very definition of ministering. I promise you that as we learn to cherish those to whom we minister, we will be blessed with eternal friendships.

Sister Eubank: The second part of Lucy Mack Smith's statement is to *watch over* one another. Recently, Sister Jean Bingham posted a message on her Facebook page asking followers to share stories of how ministering had blessed their lives. We were amazed at the examples that came in. We want to share just a few of those stories with you. These first two stories are perfect examples of sisters watching over someone who needed it. The first story comes from Kylee Beckstrom, who is from Logan, Utah:

"There were a couple of days a few weeks ago that I just felt so broken. I felt like I couldn't go on any longer. I felt like I was being tested and tried more than I could bear. I was on the phone with my mom and she knew I just needed a friend in the moment. She told me to text my Relief Society president and see if she could just go get ice cream or something with me to get my mind off the situation. I told her I didn't want to burden her with my problems, but my mom insisted. I told her I would do it, knowing I wasn't going to. I continued to just lie in my bed, feeling utterly alone. About twenty minutes later my Relief Society president texted me, saying that she was thinking about me all day and wondered if I wanted to go hang out at her place. I bawled like a baby. She was right there when I needed it. She was willing to help me through my struggles and just listen to what I was going through. She continued to text me throughout the next week just to make sure I was okay. I can't thank her enough for being so in tune with the spirit and so willing to serve others."[3]

That Relief Society president felt the Spirit and acted. That was a terrific example. Here is a second story submitted by Emily Felsted Brady from Seattle, Washington:

"We recently moved over 2,000 miles away. It has been scary and lonely. Helena Ahlstrom Jole was my visiting teacher, but she has become much more. She invited me and my children to visit parks and see the local sites. She took us to the beach and downtown Tacoma, where our children rode glass elevators up and down for a long time. We both have children with complex needs and she helped me navigate schools and listened to my concerns. I never felt like a project, and I am so grateful for her kindness and love."[4]

Aren't those beautiful examples of watching over each other? These relationships weren't just assignments on a slip of paper. They came from the Lord. Our prophet and each of our bishops, with their priesthood keys, have invited each of us to watch over one other. When we do what the Lord has asked us to do, we receive the power and authority to do it well. One of the very first scriptures new members of the Church learn is 1 Nephi 3:7—"I will go and do the things which the Lord hath commanded, for I know that the Lord giveth no commandments unto the children of men, save he shall prepare a way for them that they may accomplish the thing which he commandeth them."

Watching over one another was one of the very reasons the Relief Society was established. It all starts with getting to know the person and what they really need. Service is never going to be one size fits all. The First Presidency has directed that ministering should be led by the Spirit, flexible, and customized to the needs of those we serve. I testify the Lord will reveal to you how to minister. In small ways, you will feel promptings showing you where to go and what to do.

Sister Aburto: The third aspect of Lucy Mack Smith's statement is to *comfort* one another. Here is another beautiful story that came to Sister Bingham's Facebook page. This one is from Christina Pay, from Price, Utah.

"Our thirty-year-old daughter passed away six weeks ago. Our beliefs and knowledge of the plan of salvation have reassured and brought us comfort; however, the human body still needs to grieve, and we have discovered that grief is a very lonely place. We have felt isolated and alone since we do not have family living close by. My husband and I posted something about this loneliness on Facebook as we continued to work through the process. That evening there was a knock on the door. A young couple in our ward brought by a potted tulip. They said to plant it in our yard and when next spring comes it will remind us of our daughter. Such a sweet sentiment and beautiful reminder of the Resurrection! They stayed to visit for a while and it was obvious that they were a little out of their comfort zone as we talked about our daughter's death. Even so, they sat and listened just the same. It was the kindest thing they could have done for us and helped us to feel not so alone in our sorrow. This was true ministering. This is what the Savior would have done. Since He wasn't physically here, He touched the hearts of this sweet couple to do His bidding and they listened and ministered to us."[5]

Sister Aburto: Sister Pay, our hearts are with you, and we are so happy to have you with us. Ministering isn't so much what you do—but what you feel, and how that person feels. Do you remember the example Elder Jeffrey R. Holland shared in his April 2018 conference talk? A young mother of five collapsed suddenly. Her husband instinctively called his home teacher. This good brother and his wife immediately ran to the home. The wife stayed with the children while the home teacher drove with the young husband to the hospital. Tragically, the mother did not survive. Elder Holland says that the home teacher stayed with the distressed husband and wept with him—for a long time.[6]

One of the main points of this story wasn't that the home teacher came at the spur of the moment, but rather that the first instinct the father had was to call his home teacher. The purpose of ministering isn't for you to do something for that person every month, but instead for you to do whatever it takes so that person knows that you are a true friend, and that you will come when they need your help.

Sister Eubank: As we speak about comfort, I think about the scripture from Isaiah 61 which Jesus quoted as He began His mortal ministry in His home synagogue in Nazareth. Jesus described His own purpose as the Messiah almost entirely in terms of spiritual healing: "to bind up the brokenhearted, to proclaim liberty to the captives, and the opening of the prison to them that are bound; . . . to comfort all that mourn; . . . to give unto them beauty for ashes, the oil of joy for mourning, the garment of praise for the spirit of heaviness" (Isaiah 61:1–3). We who want to be like the Savior can comfort others in these same ways.

Sister Bingham recently shared an example of this. She told us, "My husband, Bruce, has been visiting one of our neighbors for years. Although welcoming to my husband on a personal level, the neighbor had not attended Church for many years and did not welcome a spiritual message, so Bruce was just his friend. Recently, our neighbor faced an overwhelming crisis and texted Bruce for help. Later our friend told me, 'The only thing I could think to do in my panic was to call Bruce and ask for a priesthood blessing.'" This good brother returned to activity and was welcomed with open arms by ward members.

Sister Aburto: This beautiful story shows that it doesn't always have to be a big thing. Here is a recent example from my own life. As you can imagine, I was really nervous getting ready to give my first talk in general conference. It's a scary assignment! Five-year-old Seth saw me in the hall at church and said, "I know who is speaking in conference."

"Who?" I asked.

He replied, "You! And I am praying for you, Sister Aburto."

A five-year-old ministered to me. I felt so loved. It doesn't require much for a person to feel loved. I add my witness that offering comfort is one of the most Christlike acts we can perform for others.

Sister Eubank: I love what a five-year-old can do! Along with the examples of cherishing, watching over, and comforting one another, let's talk about the next element in Lucy Mack Smith's statement: *gaining instruction.* In President Nelson's April 2018 Sunday morning conference talk, he almost begged us to learn how to receive revelation. He said, "In coming days, it will not be possible to survive spiritually without the guiding, directing, comforting, and constant influence of the Holy Ghost."[7] Gaining instruction from the Spirit is going to be critical to our future.

I know this isn't unique to me, but sometimes I'm so pressed with everything I have to do that I often don't even know what the priority *is.* I have started asking the Lord every morning, "What is one thing you want me to do today?" I'm a maximizer and I tend to think if one thing is good then five are better and ten are best. Then I'm overwhelmed. So, I've calculated if I do one thing that comes through inspiration, 365 times per year for fifty years, that will be a total of 18,250 things that the *Lord* wanted done. He has counted on me 18,250 times, and I have tried to respond. That is no small thing! One of the greatest feelings is to know when you go to bed at night that you did the best you could that day. Offer it to the Lord—"I did my best. Will you please use my offering and augment it with the grace of Jesus Christ?" And then wake up and try again the next day. I have learned so much by doing this. I had no idea how creative the Spirit can be! You want to know what some of my "one" things have been? Making a phone call, teaching kids to play Yahtzee, listening to a forgetful friend tell stories I've already heard, and once it was taking a nap!

We can also gain instruction from each other. Let me share a helpful example of this principle from Sister Bingham's Facebook page. This is Grant Emery from Crystal City, Virginia:

"When I was a young teacher, my first home teaching companion was a returned mission president. With this wonderful man, I began visiting our assigned families.

"One of the families we home taught was less-active, and after months of encouraging them, they still weren't attending church. One evening, we pulled up to their house, and my companion stopped me as I was getting out of the car. He pulled out the Doctrine and Covenants and had me read my duties as one ordained to the Aaronic Priesthood. He stopped me when I got to the part about my responsibility to call others to repentance, and told me, *that night* I would be extending an invitation to the boy my age to repent and begin attending church.

"Kindly and skillfully, my companion taught this family the importance of weekly church attendance. Then, he let me extend the invitation, never criticizing my clumsy, awkward first attempt at fulfilling my responsibility. My companion followed up by promising blessings to the family as they started to attend church.

"The family's attendance increased. With my companion's support, I talked with my fellow quorum presidency members about how we could better integrate the boy into the quorum. We made a conscious effort to bring him into the brotherhood of our quorum, and a few years later, the boy's older brother served a full-time mission.

"That first experience of calling others to repentance terrified me. Even when I did so imperfectly, my companion taught me that calling someone to repentance is more about cultivating love and faith in others than it is about identifying their shortcomings.

"For both young men and *young women,* ministering to members of their ward, especially with the help and guidance of a proactive Melchizedek Priesthood bearer or Relief Society member, prepares them for full-time missionary service and lifelong discipleship."[8]

Brother Emery gave a perfect example of a natural way to help each other as well as the youth learn how to minister. Gaining instruction from one another as well as from the Spirit allows us to fulfill our divine nature and access the power of heaven. We can be the light that leads others to the Savior as we cherish, watch over, and comfort those around us.

Sister Aburto: My sisters, you are doing great. As President Henry B. Eyring said at the April 2017 general conference: "My purpose today is both to reassure you and invigorate you. . . . Perhaps you have come to this conference . . . wondering whether your service has been acceptable. And at the same time, you may sense that there is more to do—perhaps much more!"[9]

I want to reassure you that the Lord accepts all your efforts. The announcements in general conference weren't necessarily asking us to do more—our lists are already very full! But maybe we can do the right things. The simple things. The things the Lord Himself wants done.

I learned this principle some years ago. When I was working full time out of the home, I used to make long lists of things that needed to be done on Saturday. I could never finish everything on my list. A major milestone happened when I realized I didn't need a long list for Saturday. I started to save my Saturdays for more important family time by going shopping or doing laundry on weeknights, so I would be free. My advice from my own experience is to just pick two or three things that are realistic and let the other stuff go. Spend time having fun! Enjoy your family! Do fun things with them!

Years after that realization, I started working at home. I thought: Now I'm going to have more time. I don't have meetings. I don't have to drive to work, or make a lunch to take—but I soon learned that my assumptions were not correct. Even though I tried to be disciplined in turning my computer on at eight A.M. and turning it off at five P.M., I felt that I was never done! I felt that I would never get where I wanted to be by the end of each day.

One day, I realized I will never be done. My lists will never be finished. It isn't possible. I want to tell every woman what I have learned. You don't have to do it all, and you are never done, and you can be okay with that, and you can accept that. Do what you can each day, ask the Lord to fill in the gaps, and then, a new day starts, and you begin again. That is part of the beauty of being disciples of Jesus Christ—that we are never done, that there is always something else to do, and that there is always room for improvement.

Sister Eubank: Let me share one more quote from President Eyring: "It's natural to feel some inadequacy when we consider what the Lord has called us to do. In fact, if you told me that you feel perfectly capable of fulfilling your . . . duties, I might worry that you do not understand them. On the other hand, if you told me that you feel like giving up because the task is too far beyond your abilities, then I would want to help you understand how the Lord magnifies and strengthens [His servants] to do things they never could have done alone."[10]

In Doctrine and Covenants 64:29, 33–34, we are both re-assured and invigorated: "Wherefore, as ye are agents, ye are on the Lord's errand; and whatever ye do according to the will of the Lord is the Lord's business. . . . Wherefore, be not weary in well-doing, for ye are laying the foundation of a great work. And out of small things proceedeth that which is great. Behold, the Lord requireth the heart and a willing mind; and the willing and obedient shall eat the good of the land of Zion in these last days."

As we seek the Lord's will and strive to do it, we are assured that every small effort is accepted. All the Lord asks of us is a heart full of love and willingness to share that love. We've all made covenants to "mourn with those that mourn" and "comfort those that stand in need of comfort" (Mosiah 18:9). But that doesn't mean to run ourselves ragged. Doing *better* doesn't always mean doing *more*. And if you do just one inspired thing each day, you are nevertheless the Lord's agent.

Now, let us ask *you* a question: What are you going to do to minister in a higher, holier way? We've talked about being Spirit-led, flexible, customized to the need—what is going to be different than before? Think about this question. Feel free to write something down.

Following the example of Jesus Christ will help you know how to move forward. "The Savior is our example in everything—not only in what we should do but *why* we should do it (see Ephesians 5:2). 'His life on earth was [an] invitation to us—to raise our sights a little higher, to forget our own problems and [to] reach out to others.'"[11]

As we cherish one another's gifts as well as our differences, as we watch over one another with genuine care, as we comfort each other in our challenges, and as we are willing to learn from one another while gaining instruction from the Holy Ghost, we will be prepared to sit down in heaven together. May that heavenly experience begin for us in this mortal life; may we enjoy the happiness described by Nephi, at the time the Savior appeared to the Nephites in ancient America:

"And it came to pass that there was no contention in the land, because of the love of God which did dwell in the hearts of the people. And there were no envyings, nor strifes . . . and surely there could not be a happier people among all the people who had been created by the hand of God. . . .

"They were in one, the children of Christ, and heirs to the kingdom of God" (4 Nephi 1:15–17).

I want to bear my testimony. Our Heavenly Father loves us with a love that we cannot actually conceive of. But we feel it closely with the people that we love. And when someone passes away and dies, when we lose somebody, and we feel that unbearableness of it because we love them so much and we want to be with them—He feels like that about every single one of us. And He wants us back. He has let us be siblings to each other so we can help each other, put our arms around each other, stop worrying about how different we are, and instead bless one another's lives. And as President Kevin J Worthen said, the most important thing we can do to bless each other's lives is not just to care for one another and be kind and be nice, but to help each other make covenants, so that we can be the absolute happiest when we return to our Heavenly Father and Heavenly Mother.

I know it's hard, I know life is complex, and I know things get in the way. But I testify that the Lord Jesus Christ gives us power and strength day by day if we will just ask and if we will use our agency to act. This testimony has become the very linchpin of my life—it's how I'm trying to live my life. And I see you trying to live it yourselves, and I am so grateful to be linked with sisters around this whole globe who are trying for those same goals. In my work, I see very difficult things, and those things happen because the love of men and women toward God and each other has waxed cold. You are the reason that I can get up every morning—because of the faith and the hope and the comfort and the caring that you bring to everybody else. I bear my witness that the Lord will help us as we try to live His law.

Sister Aburto: I also would like to share my testimony with all of you. I want you to know that I know that we are daughters of our Heavenly Father who loves us. I know that He is mindful of each of us personally. He knows each of us, and He knows the desires of our hearts. He knows that we are willing to listen to Him. And this new way of ministering, this new, higher and holier way of ministering, will allow us to show Him how much we love Him. I know that we have a Savior and a Redeemer, and that He came to this earth so He could actually feel and go through the things that we have to go through so He can come and give us His mercy and His love. I know, sisters, that sometimes we may think that it's hard to take another step, but I know if we have faith in our Savior, and in the power that we can receive from Him, we will have the strength that we need to keep going. Please turn your heart to Him. Let Him guide you through the Spirit, and you will know the things that you need to do each day. We pray for you, sisters. We love you. And we are so thankful to you for everything that you do to minister to each other, to strengthen each other in the Lord, and for everything that you do to be a light to the world. I know that we are in the true church and that we have a prophet today.

Value beyond Measure

Our Relationship with an All-Knowing and Loving Heavenly Father

Mary Williams

President Spencer W. Kimball declared, "God is your Father. He loves you. He and your mother in heaven value you beyond any measure. . . . You are unique. One of a kind, made of eternal intelligence which gives you claim upon eternal life."[1] Sister Joy D. Jones teaches, "As the Savior lifts us to higher ground, we can see more clearly not only who we are but also that we are closer to Him than we ever imagined."[2] Elder Dieter F. Uchtdorf observes, "I believe that every man, woman, and child has felt the call of heaven at some point in his or her life. Deep within us is a longing to somehow reach past the veil and embrace Heavenly Parents we once knew and cherished."[3] How can we recognize Heavenly Father's love for us? How are we each special, unique, and valued? How does our knowledge of God's love for us guide our daily choices and actions?

My dear sisters, it is honor to be with you. I have prayed with all the energy of my heart that I might impart those things Heavenly Father would have you hear. I sense there are those that feel burdened and long for the comfort, peace, and the healing power that comes from a loving Heavenly Father. My prayer is that the Spirit will provide answers to the yearnings of your heart.

I would like to talk about the most powerful knowledge you can possess and it is this: you are a child of God, a beloved daughter of our Heavenly Father. Primary children sing, "I Am a Child of God";[4] weekly the Young Women proclaim, "We are daughters of our Heavenly Father, who loves us, and we love Him";[5] and latter-day prophets and apostles testify that "each [of us] is a beloved spirit son or daughter of heavenly parents, and, as such, each has a divine nature and destiny."[6]

What is the power of knowing you are a child of God? President Boyd K. Packer reminds us, "Spiritually you are of noble birth, the offspring of the King of Heaven. . . . However, many generations in your mortal ancestry, no matter what race or people you represent, the pedigree of your spirit can be written on a single line. You are a child of God!"[7]

Being a child of God means you are loved perfectly and known perfectly. He knows you intimately, He knows your name, He understands every struggle, heartache, and loss you will ever experience—and because of that, He knows how to bring healing, comfort, and peace. He will never abandon you. He cannot and will not. His very nature and purpose are to walk beside you in love.

Because of your divine heritage, you are blessed with potential and value beyond measure. With that knowledge, you should never think of yourself as a nothing. You have a perfect spiritual gene pool from Heavenly Parents with the potential to become as they are.

Some of you may find it difficult to feel that you are a beloved daughter of Heavenly Father or that He is even there. You may struggle with your value and worth. You may even question if your life matters. My dear sisters, if you question His reality or feel unworthy of His love simply ask as the words of the Primary hymn suggest:

"Heavenly Father, are you really there? [And do you love me?]"

And you will hear:

"Speak, [I am] listening / You are [my] child / [My] love now surrounds you. [I hear] your prayer."[8]

Sister Joy D. Jones, Primary General President, tells of a sister from India and the impact of coming to knowing she was a daughter of a loving Heavenly Father:

"'Before I started investigating the Church, I didn't really feel that I was very special. I was just one of many people, and my society and culture didn't really teach me that I had any value as an individual. When . . . I learned that I was a daughter of our Heavenly Father, it changed me. Suddenly I felt so special—God had actually created me and had created my soul and my life with value and purpose. . . .

"'I was always trying to prove to others that I was someone special. But when I learned the truth, that I am a daughter of God, I didn't have to prove anything to anyone. I knew that I was special. . . . Don't ever think that you are nothing.'"[9]

Our greatest yearning in this life is to be loved perfectly. That yearning comes because we once felt that perfect love from our Heavenly Mother and Father. Elder Dieter F. Uchtdorf observed, "I believe that every man, woman, and child has felt the call of heaven at some point in his or her life. Deep within us is a longing to somehow reach past the veil and embrace Heavenly Parents we once knew and cherished."[10]

While in nursing school, I came to more fully understand

the power of love. In my pediatric class, I wrote a "Maternal Deprivation" paper. The purpose of the paper was to review the research on why institutionalized infants often failed to grow and even live. Researchers questioned why infants who were being fed and sheltered failed to survive. After much study, they concluded that it was because of the lack of a mother's love.

As a mother's love is needed for our physical bodies to thrive and grow, when we do not feel the love of Heavenly Father, our spirits likewise fail to grow to their full potential. In the Book of Mormon, Lehi describes God's love as "most sweet" (1 Nephi 8:11) and Nephi indicates it is "most desirable above all things" and the "most joyous to the soul" (1 Nephi 11:22–23).

Elder Melvin J. Ballard, an apostle in this dispensation, describes the power of God's love. In the dreams of the night, he found himself in the temple and was told he would have the privilege to meet a glorious Personage:

"As I entered the door, I saw . . . the most glorious Being my eyes have ever beheld or that I ever conceived existed in all the eternal worlds. . . . He took me into his arms and kissed me, pressed me to his bosom, and blessed me, until the marrow of my bones seemed to melt! . . . The feeling that I had in the presence of him who hath all things in his hands, to have his love, his affection, and his blessing was such that if I ever can receive that of which I had but a foretaste, I would give all that I am, all that I ever hope to be, to feel what I then felt!"[11]

If you question your worth or worthiness to receive that love, read what President Thomas S. Monson said as he spoke to the women of the Church:

"My dear sisters, your Heavenly Father loves you—each of you. That love never changes. It is not influenced by your appearance, by your possessions, or by the amount of money you have in your bank account. It is not changed by your talents and abilities. It is simply there. It is there for you when you are sad or happy, discouraged or hopeful. God's love is there for you whether you feel you deserve love. It is simply always there."[12]

Might I suggest a few ways that you can enhance your ability to feel God's love. First, seek to know and trust God. President Russell M. Nelson testifies, "Something powerful happens when a child of God seeks to know more about Him and His Beloved Son."[13] That kind of knowing is far more than knowing facts or stories about Him. As we follow in the covenant path by strict obedience to His commandments, we will come to know Him and His love. Each covenant and commandment brings us closer to Him and endows us with power and blessings, and we come to trust Him. We are promised blessings for Sabbath-day worship, blessings for temple attendance, blessings for scripture study, blessings for paying of tithes and offerings, blessings for missionary work, blessings for ministering, blessings of doing family history, and the list goes on and on. Read President Nelson's promised blessings of reading the Book of Mormon daily—are these not blessings we desire most? "I promise that as you prayerfully study the Book of Mormon *every day,* you will make better decisions— *every day.* I promise that as you ponder what you study, the windows of heaven will open, and you will receive answers to your own questions and direction for your own life. I promise that as you daily immerse yourself in the Book of Mormon, you can be immunized against the evils of the day, even the gripping plague of pornography and other mind-numbing addictions."[14]

Coming to know Him and feeling His love happens when we are completely honest in our prayers. When you talk with

Heavenly Father, are you authentic in your feelings and your struggles? Satan desires that you not communicate with Heavenly Father and tells you lies. He tells you to stop talking with Heavenly Father because you are unworthy. Satan tells you God has withdrawn and is punishing you for what you have done. He plants in your mind the thoughts, *Why am I having adversity? Haven't I kept all the commandments and done what I have been asked?* When difficulties come, Satan tells you, "If there were a Heavenly Father, this would not be happening. Surely there is no God." My dear sisters, do not let the deceitfulness and lies of Satan prevent you from having the most endearing and powerful relationship possible.

The key, my sisters, to feeling God's love, knowing Him, and trusting Him is to share your real feelings and struggles with Him, whether they be anger, hurt, pain, loneliness, rejection, frustration—or joy, happiness, and gratitude. Brigham Young suggests, "Cling to him, make friends with him . . . Open and keep open a communication with [him]."[15]

I experienced a time in my life when communication with Heavenly Father became very authentic. I expressed my anger, my fears, my anxiety, my frustration, and my pain. I learned, as never before, that expressing what we may view as negative emotions does not cause Him or His love to withdraw.

One of the things I feared most in my life was cancer. I cared for my dear sister who died at the age of forty-one from liver and pancreatic cancer. I watched the debilitating effects of cancer and chemotherapy. I cared for my father as he died from pancreatic cancer. Then I got cancer. I remember questioning Heavenly Father with great intensity as to why the thing I feared most was happening to me. I remember saying, "This is not fair.

This cannot be." Before starting chemotherapy, I received a blessing. I was told Heavenly Father desired to heal me but it would take time. I was told I would experience angels on both sides of the veil ministering to me. I was promised I would have spiritual experiences that would strengthen me and help me to know of God's love. I awoke early the day I was to start chemo with overwhelming feelings of fear and anxiety. As I lay in my bed, I heard my sister's voice, who had passed away from cancer, say, "Mary, I know how frightening this can be and how hard this is for you. I will be with you today to comfort you." And she was; I felt her the entire day.

Sometimes we feel that God's love means everything will be just how we want it without struggles, every day will be perfect, every prayer will be answered just how we want, when we want. My dear sisters, our Heavenly Father wants us to become all we can and that cannot happen without difficulties and struggles. It may seem strange to say that the thing I feared most—cancer—I now view as my friend. None of us likes adversity. However, if we seek to learn what Heavenly Father would have us learn, rather than becoming angry and bitter and withdrawing from our greatest source of strength, our struggles will be a source of growth, strength, and understanding. My cancer allowed me to feel God's love in abundance, experience His comforting Spirit, know the reality of loving, ministering angels on both sides of the veil, appreciate the gift of life, and gain the sure knowledge that Heavenly Father is always there in rain and sunshine. Now I have the blessing to minister to those with cancer.

We will feel God's love as we look daily for the tender mercies and miracles designed uniquely for us. When President Henry B. Eyring's children were young, he started the habit of writing about the blessings that had happened during the day. Before he wrote, he would ponder this question: "Have I seen the hand of God reaching out to touch us or our children or our family?" He notes, "As I kept at it, something began to happen. As I would cast my mind over the day, I would see evidence of what God had done for one of us that I had not recognized in the busy moments of the day. . . . [It] allowed God to show me what He had done."[16]

Take moments each day to pause, see Heavenly Father's hand in every detail of your life, and remember Him. It will influence your decisions and keep your priorities straight, whether setting an alarm on your phone to remind you to remember Heavenly Father or doing as Elder Brian K. Taylor suggested when he described the healing power of saying ten times per day, "I am a child of God."[17]

Elder W. Craig Zwick recounts a tender incident that reflects how a young man remembered Heavenly Father. While four-wheeling with a friend, the vehicle he was driving flipped over and pinned him under its four-hundred-pound frame. Even though all efforts were made to rescue and save him, the young man passed away. While at the hospital, a police officer entered the room and handed his cell phone to his grieving mother. As she took the phone, an audible alarm sounded. She opened the phone and saw on her now-dead son's daily alarm: "Remember to put Jesus Christ at the center of your life today."[18]

Perhaps the most powerful way we feel our Heavenly Father's love is ministering to the one as the Savior would do. In the April 2018 general conference, we were asked to increase our efforts to minister. Our Brigham Young University Women's Conference theme invites us to "strengthen one another in the Lord." As we pray daily for opportunities to minister and strengthen others, we will feel God's love.

In the Book of Mormon we are taught that charity is "the pure love of Christ" and "never faileth" (Moroni 7:47, 46). Elder Dale G. Renlund teaches, "Only when we see through Heavenly Father's eyes can we be filled with 'the pure love of Christ' (Moroni 7:47)."[19]

We are counseled to "pray unto the Father with all the energy of heart, that ye may be filled with this love" (Moroni 7:48).

Filled with charity, we become His hands and His heart to bring healing, comfort, and love. When we feel the promptings of the Spirit and follow them, we will feel His love, be given His words, and be told how to uniquely minister to each individual. We will see them as Heavenly Father sees them.

A number of years ago while serving as a Relief Society president, I was asked to visit a sister who was experiencing serious health problems. I did not know her, but I had been told of frequent family conflicts which necessitated the police coming to her home. As I went to her home, her daughter was hesitant to let me in. In fact, she boldly stood in the doorway. I introduced myself as the Relief Society president. There was dead silence. Finally I said, "I'm a nurse and I have come to see if I can help." Slowly, I was allowed in. I was introduced to someone with a cigarette in one hand and a can of beer in the other hand. As I sat there, I felt the strongest impression that I should tell her Heavenly Father loved her. I thought to myself, *Sure, that will go over like a bomb and you'll be thrown out.*

I eventually gained the courage to give the message Heavenly Father wanted her to know. I pulled my chair up close to hers, looked her in the eyes, and said, "Pat, I want you to know Heavenly Father loves you." I felt the love of Heavenly Father for her fill my whole being. I saw her as Heavenly Father did—as a beloved daughter with of divine worth. Her eyes filled with tears, and she said, "Me?" and I said, "Yes, you." That day my relationship changed with her and I was changed forever by feeling Heavenly Father's love for her. I have been her visiting teacher for over thirteen years. Most often as I enter her home, she is still sitting in a chair with a cigarette in one hand and a can of beer in the other hand. However, that never changes the love Heavenly Father has for her, nor the love I feel for her. Recently she had open-heart surgery and desired a priesthood blessing. As I visited her in the hospital following her surgery, she said, with tears in her eyes, "That blessing saved my life." She knew Heavenly Father loved her. And what happened to her daughter? Several years ago, I was invited to her daughter's baptism. Her countenance radiated, and as she came up out of the water, her words were, "I am clean." Heavenly Father's love is a source of miracles to others and to each of us.

My dear sisters, I bear testimony that you are a child of God, and He loves you. You are created in His image with a noble birthright. Your worth is beyond measure. As you seek to know Heavenly Father through honest and open communication, you will find Him. His love for you can be seen in daily miracles and God's tender mercies that reflect His knowledge of every detail of your life. You are never beyond the reach of His love. As you seek to minister and strengthen others in the Lord, you will be filled with the pure love of Christ and taste of the sweetness of that love. When you cry out, "Heavenly Father, are you there—and do you love me?" I bear testimony that He is; His love is simply and always there.

WAITING UPON THE LORD

Annalece Boothe Misiego

I really only know about two things, and I'm going to share them with you. The first thing that I know for sure is that we have a Father in Heaven who loves us. What do we want for the people that we love? We want them to be happy, right? There's even a scripture, I know you're all thinking of it, in 2 Nephi 2, "Men are"—or men exist—"that they might have joy" (2 Nephi 2:25). Right? That's one of the things that I know. I *know* that He wants us to be happy because I've had experiences in my life where I didn't deserve to be happy but I was. I know that He wants happiness for His children.

The other thing that I know is that Jesus Christ is every good thing. He carries us and He sits with us and He will lift us when we need to be lifted, and we all have times when that becomes necessary.

This is an incredible gathering of women! I can't help but think about all the different things that we are experiencing right now. We can look around at each other and think, *I'm going to draw strength from you because of what you are going through and I'm going to draw strength from you because of what you are fighting and beating.* We've got it all, but Jesus Christ can make all of that easier. He can't take away the pain completely, but He can make it easier to bear.

Growing up, my parents would often ask, "Have you read your scriptures? Have you prayed?" I never said it aloud, but I always asked myself, *Why? Why do I need to pray or read?* One day I decided to kneel down and ask, "Why?" And the answer that came to me was a three-word sentence: "To get ready." *To get ready for what?* I wondered to my sixteen-year-old self. But every time, I would ask why I needed to do those small things, and every time I asked, the same answer came: "To get ready."

When I was a young adult, I was called on a mission to Rochester, New York. I was ecstatic. I knew that the mission field was where I truly belonged. But on my second day in the Missionary Training Center, I was sent home by the MTC doctor because he didn't feel that I was well enough to be there. I had had a surgery prior to my entering the MTC and had received clearance from my surgeon, but the MTC doctor didn't agree, so home I went. That was when the answer to my "why?" question I'd asked over and over again started to make sense.

After some time at home, I reentered the MTC and loved every second of it. I mean, where else do you get to study the gospel of Jesus Christ all day *and* eat all the cold cereal you could ever desire? That was my heaven.

I entered the mission field and was placed with a companion that had only been in the field for two transfers. I'm sure our mission president was wondering what exactly he was doing, but it didn't take long for Sister Call and I to realize why we were put together as the newbies. We were exactly alike. We had the time of our lives together.

Sister Call is really athletic, so we would wake up at 6:30 and she would run and I would shuffle along behind her. She would run about a block ahead of me and turn around and come back to meet me. Anyway, one morning in August, we got home from a run and I looked down and realized that my kneecap was sitting on my shin. It had just fallen down and couldn't get back up. It seemed like a pretty serious problem, but what could I do? I bought a large bottle of Advil and a solid supply of Diet Coke with Lime and pushed through. Truthfully, I knew that if I made a big deal of it, I would be sent home again—and I had already done that! The words entered my mind again: "To get ready," and I knew I was ready to take this on. The words penned by President Gordon B. Hinckley's father, Bryant, rang in my mind: "Forget yourself and go to work."[1] So that's what I did.

I was transferred to a new companion who was dealing with some really heavy things in her life, and I thought *Perfect! I can put all of my energy into her and I'll just forget that my kneecap is on my shin.*

We got a phone call in mid-November from our mission president and he said, "Sister Boothe, I need you and Sister Colbert to come over to the mission home tonight." I said, "President, we have a dinner appointment," which was not common in our mission. "We cannot come." I knew that he knew about my knee. I said, "We can't come because we're busy." He said, "Well, come after."

"But that will be after curfew!" to which he said, "Sister Boothe. I am the mission president. I know that."

I felt so sick during the entire dinner appointment, and when it was over, we went to the mission home. When we got there, the mission president said, "Let me see your knee." At this point it wasn't recognizable as a knee because the swelling was so intense and my kneecap was sitting about four inches lower than was to be expected.

He said, "That's really bad."

I said, "I know, but *please* don't send me home!"

He said, "You have to go home." And the next day, I was home and heartbroken.

I had surgery immediately and was told that it would take nine months to recover. I was scheduled to reenter the mission field for the third time at the beginning of September. I was in my orthopedist's office receiving my final okay to reenter the mission field only days before I was scheduled to fly out to New York. He did final X-rays and scans and then he came back into the exam room with a long face and said, "I don't know how this happened, but everything that was intact when we opened you up is now completely shredded. We have to do another surgery. You can't go on a mission anymore."

I called my mission president that night and through many tears I said: "President! This is not how this is supposed to go! I want to have doors slammed in my face! I want that so bad!" Then he said something that changed my life. He said, "This is your chance to dedicate the rest of your life to missionary work. I hope you will."

When I was told that I couldn't return to full-time missionary service, I felt completely forgotten. I felt like God had just left and I couldn't figure out why, because I was doing what I thought He wanted me to do. I quickly found out that I didn't feel this way because He had left, but because I had stopped looking for His goodness in my life.

Three months later, my mom was diagnosed with cancer. I

got to sleep by her hospital bed many nights. I sat there, looking at her with no hair, and I thought to myself, *Heavenly Father, you did this for me, didn't you? You made it so I couldn't go back into the mission field so that I could be here for her.* That was when I started seeing Him and finding Him in the strangest of places.

A few years later, I met my dear husband and we started a wild adventure. We had a baby quickly after getting married, and when she was two years old and I was sixteen weeks along with our second child, I woke up one morning to iron a white shirt for my husband. He works for the Church, so I iron white shirts more than I care to think about. I woke up at six on a Tuesday morning in August and I went to iron his shirt and I ironed the entire thing with my hand—not holding an iron—with *just* my hand. When I finished, I held the shirt up and thought to myself, *What is the matter with you?* I plugged in the iron and did the whole thing again and then I walked into the bathroom where he was getting ready and I sort of shoved it at him and I said very angrily, "We've got to start sending these shirts out!" and went back to bed. He just kindly left the house without another word because he is a really good person.

My daughter and I went to run some errands later that day and she wanted a happy meal, so we got in the line at the McDonald's drive-through, and the employee greeted us through the speaker and said, "Welcome to McDonald's! Can I take your order?" And I couldn't talk. He said it again, and I tried to speak, but nothing came out of my mouth. It was then that I realized that I couldn't read the menu board. We left, and I got on the interstate (obviously). I called my husband, but he didn't answer because he was in a meeting. Then I called my dad, who picked right up. I'm not sure what I was thinking—I mean, I couldn't talk, but

I was calling him on the phone. In our fifteen-minute conversation, I got out five words. One of those words was "point," but it came out very stuttered. It is a miracle that my father understood any of it. "Point" makes reference to the "Point of the Mountain" between Draper and Lehi that you drive by as you enter Utah County, and with that one word, he knew where I was.

The next thing I remember, my brother Mark and our friend Bradley found me in a parking lot and they gave me a blessing. In the blessing, Bradley said that I would be sustained in my current state until I could get the help that I needed.

I had meat in the trunk and I tried to tell my brother to put the meat in the freezer after he dropped me off at the emergency room, but I couldn't talk. He asked, "Meat?"

"Meat." In my jumbled thoughts, I was so worried about the chicken going bad.

I entered the emergency room and the doctor told my family to take me home to have me sleep it off. Then he had the nerve to ask, "Does she do this kind of thing often?" What? Pretend I can't talk? No! I love to talk. Twenty-four hours after being admitted to the ER, my parents and family finally convinced the doctor to do an MRI. With the MRI, the doctors discovered three blood clots on my brain. Because so much time had passed, those parts of my brain were already dead. Those blood clots were on the language center of my brain, which is why I had lost my ability to verbalize.

I lay there in that hospital bed, mostly sleeping, but every time I was awake I prayed so hard that Heavenly Father would let me say kind words to my husband just one more time. I wanted so badly to have one more chance to tell my husband and daughter how much I loved them.

Three days after the initial stroke, I woke up from one of my deep sleeps and stumbled over three words. My mom was sitting there and when I spoke, there was much rejoicing because they didn't know if I'd ever speak again. I finally learned what the Spirit had been telling me my whole life. I realized what I had been "getting ready" for. I knew it with my knee injury and my mother's cancer, but lying there in my hospital bed, the seriousness of this stroke hit me. This was going to be big. This was going to be a long recovery. I had to relearn how to speak and read. I didn't know if I could sing, and I wasn't sure that I wanted to live if I couldn't sing. I didn't know if I was still pregnant. Many people who have strokes lose their babies, and only forty-five out of every 100,000 people have strokes like mine, and only 10 percent of those patients recover fully. I was incredibly blessed and let me tell you why.

I was incredibly blessed because of prayer. The prayers! I cannot begin to understand how prayer works, but I know that it does. I know that because I'm standing here. I cannot begin to understand how the Savior feels everything that we feel, but I know He does because He stood by me and carried me through my recovery, and because of that, I am standing here today.

Waiting upon the Lord means patience, right? That's probably what you thought you would hear from me, but sorry, you're not going to. Waiting on the Lord means patience, but waiting *upon* the Lord means something very different. How many of you have ever waited tables? That is fun, isn't it? Do you spend a lot of time patiently waiting when you are a waiter or a waitress? No. Your job is about serving. Waiting *upon* the Lord means to serve Him. Be patient, yes, because He is everlastingly patient with us.

We tend to rebel. We tend to forget, but He never does that. He will wait for us for eternity, and He will forever wait upon us.

I want everyone to find their heartbeat. That is service, my friends. He keeps that beating. How about that scripture in Mosiah 2:21? "[God] has created you from the beginning, and is preserving you from day to day, by lending you breath, that ye may live and move and do according to your own will, and even supporting you from one moment to another."

Wow. He is amazing. But what are we doing for Him? He gives us every breath. What are we doing in return? We can develop faith, hope, and charity. But how? We hear that all the time, but how are we going to really develop those attributes?

We can develop faith and hope by being patient and knowing and trusting—even when we don't quite believe—that He is in control. It's that mustard seed that Alma talks about. Just try. Just try a little and you will find great things. We can serve Him by learning of Him. Think of when someone takes the time to get to know who you are, gets to know your likes, dislikes, etc. How does that make you feel? It makes us feel good, right? Don't you think it makes Heavenly Father feel good when we try to get to know Him? So how do we get to know Him? We already have that answer. Study and pray. Learning of Him shows Him that we *love* Him. Developing a relationship of prayer shows Him that we *trust* Him. Acting on all of this shows Him that we *believe* Him.

We can serve Him by doing what He asks. We have very recently been asked by our prophet, President Russell M. Nelson, to start ministering. So send that text message, take that treat. We are all going to make fools of ourselves in our lives, so just get over that. We have to get over ourselves so that we can reach out, because that's what we've been asked to do by a prophet of God. We've got to do it. We've got to help Him. We've got to serve Him. He can do His work without us, but He is allowing us to help. Let's not miss out on this opportunity.

We have to up our game, my friends. Remember Elder Jeffrey R. Holland, who recently said, "The great thing about the gospel is that we get credit for *trying.*"[2] So when you tell someone that you're going to pray for them, stop right then, drop whatever you're doing, and pray. Our mission president would say, "Stay on your knees until you the feel the love of God." Stay there. It took me a while the first time, but now, every time I get on my knees, I feel His love.

How about our study game? We've got to make some decisions about our scripture study and our commitment to that. You know, "Hour of Power," scripture journals—there are all kinds of pens that won't bleed through your scripture pages. We have all the tools, but we have to put them to use. We have to try. That's all; we've just got to try.

We have to up our temple attendance game. In 2009, Elder Richard G. Scott said that fourteen years earlier, he had decided to attend the temple every week and if he missed a week, he would go twice the next week. He said it had made all the difference in his life.[3] When I heard these words back in 2009, I thought, *Well, he can do that because he's not in college. I definitely don't have time for that right now.* But his words have followed me, and every once in a while they cross my mind and I find myself making excuses for that stage in my life. *Well, Elder Scott didn't have little children when he started doing this. Elder Scott's office is practically next door to the temple! It's easy for him!* Then, at the beginning of this year, I was kneeling down and asked Heavenly

Father, "Tell me what you want me to do. How can I be better this year?" and Elder Scott's talk paraded right through my mind. My initial thought was *I have three small children now! I can't make that happen.* But we can always make it happen. Going to the temple more often has changed my life. It has made all the difference, just as Elder Scott said it would. I understand that now.

We just have to up our game. We have to up our game in so many ways. We've already talked about service. Just get out there! Just do something for someone, because it is amazing how healed we become when we serve someone else, and as Elder Holland said, "You get credit for trying."[4] We're going to fail. But we are going to be awesome too, and we get credit for all of that.

We've got to let the gospel sink deeper into us. What we've been asked to do has to live and breathe in our souls and in our hearts. I want to share one more quote from Elder Holland that he gave at the April 2018 BYU commencement. He said, "This is the Church of the happy endings. Troubles need never be permanent nor fatal. Darkness always yields to light. The sun always rises. Faith, hope, and charity will always triumph in the end. Furthermore, they will triumph all along the way."[5]

God is great. And He can and will make us great, but we have to get ready.

Our Savior's Love

Susan L. Gong

Wonderful things happen when righteous, faithful, open-to-the-Spirit women gather. Because of what we'll learn here, we will be different. We take away a surer sense of God's love for us, and that gives us strength to do what is most important and special—the small and simple things we do to lift, serve, and minister to one another.

The change from "visiting teaching to ministering in a high and holier way"[1] invites us to think more deeply about the new commandment that the Savior gave His disciples, "As I have loved you, . . . love one another" (John 13:34). I want to share three observations about what it might mean to love as Jesus loves.

UNDERSTAND

First, Jesus knows the heart of every daughter or son of God. In the New Testament, we see that He understands the essential nature of every person He meets. He knows Nathanael is a man without guile (see John 1:46–51). He knows Nicodemus, the Pharisee who sneaks in in the middle of the night, is truly seeking to understand (see John 3:1–13). And from the beginning He understands that Peter—impetuous, hopeful, vulnerable, two-steps-forward-one-step-back Peter—has it within him to lead the Church, else why would Christ, on their very first meeting, give him the name Cephas, meaning "the Rock"? (John 1:42).

Christ knows the heart of the Samaritan woman: "Thou hast well said, I have no husband: for thou hast had five husbands; and he whom thou now hast is not thy husband" (John 4:17–18). Those words must have been spoken with incredible tenderness because they evoke such a humble response, perhaps one full of wonder. "Sir, I perceive that thou art a prophet" (John 4:19).

He knows the hearts of His persecutors: "Father, forgive them; for they know not what they do" (JST, Luke 23:35).

There is healing, there is hope in just being known, just being understood. Perhaps you instinctively know the hearts of those you minister to. Perhaps you have that incredible gift of discernment. I do not. So if I am to love as Jesus would love, what do I need to do? I need to learn to listen.

When Elder Gong and I lived in Hong Kong, our apartment was located on one of the busiest streets in one of the busiest cities in the world. It was often hard to hear Gerrit unless we stood face-to-face. One day in frustration, Gerrit said, "Sweetheart, when we're next in Salt Lake will you please have your hearing tested?" I obligingly visited an audiologist who, after testing my hearing, proclaimed, "Mrs. Gong, I have good news and bad news. The good news is your hearing is perfect. The bad news is that may mean you have a listening problem, and there's not much I can do about that."

So I am on notice—I need to learn to listen better. I need to put down my electronic devices. I need to shut out the distractions and turn off the little voice in my head that's constantly reminding me of all of the things on my "to do" list. And then listen with my heart, to understand not just what someone is saying, but who it is I'm talking to: a child of God. I need to listen for that.

I'm discovering that listening means not just hearing the other person, but listening to the Holy Ghost as well. The Holy Ghost helps us ask inspired questions that lead us to greater understanding.

FEEL COMPASSION

A second observation from the scriptures about how Jesus loves us is that compassion always accompanies Christ's understanding of our hearts. He has compassion on the blind (see John 9:1–7), on the widow of Nain (see Luke 7:12–18),[2] on lepers (see Luke 17:12–19), on the brother of Jared (Ether 3:6–13), on one possessed with a devil (see Mark 5:1–13; Luke 4:33–37), and, multiple times, He has compassion on the multitude (see 3 Nephi 17:7, 9; Matthew 9:36, 14:14, 15:32; Mark 8:2). From the cross, He voices compassion for Mary, His mother (see John 19:26–27). Surely it is through His compassion that "he hath borne our grief" (Isaiah 53:4).

Compassion is at the heart of Christ's parables: The parable of the debtor (see Luke 7:41–43), the Good Samaritan (Luke 10:30–37), the father of the prodigal son (see Luke 15:11–32), all exhibit compassion.

For most of us, compassion requires imagination and intention. In our spheres of ministering we can strive to feel how it really feels

- to wrangle adorable and demanding preschoolers day in and day out.
- to be a divorced mom reentering the workforce after many years.

- to be ninety and alone.
- to be the returning prodigal.
- to have been abandoned.
- to receive a diagnosis of cancer.
- to have been abused.
- to have lost a child to illness.
- to have lost a child to the world.

As Christians we are called to feel the pain of others. In this we truly "bear one another's burdens" (Mosiah 18:8). When we have compassion—true empathy—something wondrous happens. We begin to know how to help.

BLESS

This is my third observation about how Jesus loves. Having taken upon Himself our infirmities, He knows how to succor us. Having felt our fear, our want, our loneliness, our hunger, our hurt, He responds to our specific need. He comforts, supplies, feeds, heals, nurtures, teaches, and blesses us.

Like the Good Samaritan, when Christ finds us suffering, He has compassion on us, He comes to us, binds our wounds, and brings us to the inn and cares for us (see Luke 10:33–34).

And the Church is the inn where we, like the innkeeper, are called upon to minister to each other until the Master returns.

Know the heart. Feel compassion. Bless. This is the Savior's pattern of ministering—and it can be ours.

I recently lost a dear friend who lived by this pattern. At her funeral her daughter said, "My mother was good at everything important and special. She wanted everyone to have their story known. She paid notice in the most significant ways. How can you give up on yourself when your mom is this most profound person who sees you as you are and still believes in you?"

Another eulogy described this dear Christlike sister like this: "She was the giver of thoughtful gifts, the rescuer of stranded souls, a healer of broken hearts, a polisher of tarnished halos. She was the kind of person who always held the mirror at the most flattering angle. A woman of substance. She was observant of human need. Her response to suffering was always to ease the burden. Hers was love unfeigned."

As I hear the prophet call us to a higher, holier form of ministry, I think of my friend. We are being asked to love as she loved—to be good at what is special and important.

But where do we get the patience, insight, imagination, courage, and strength to love like this?

In December I had the blessing of attending the Salt Lake Temple with a recently endowed friend, a sister I've known since elementary school. Life has presented her with many challenges, and her connection with the Church has sometimes been tenuous, though I believe she has always had a spark of the gospel in her heart.

As we walked the corridors of that magnificent temple, she stopped at every painting of the Savior, reached toward it, then bowed her head and touched her heart. In the celestial room she prayed fervently—having finally come to the House of the Lord, she was in no hurry to leave. On our way home we walked through a bookstore, each of us browsing different sections.

Coming up behind me she whispered, "Susan, you've got to see this! Someone has painted a picture of me!" We rounded a corner. She pointed to this beautiful image created by Brian Kershisnik.[3] "That's me!" She exclaimed. "That's just how I feel!"

She Will Find What Is Lost, by Brian T. Kershisnik

Loved.

Blessed.

Sisters, I testify that because we are loved with the "matchless bounty of the [Savior's] love" (Alma 26:15), with the infinite love of our Heavenly Father, through their love we can come to understand one another, have compassion for one another, and bless one another, in every way that is important and special. "We love him, because he first loved us" (1 John 4:19). Because He loves us, we can learn to love and minister to one another. The Holy Ghost will help us know how.

This glorious gospel is true. It is powerful. It is beautiful and it is important.

"Strengthen One Another in the Lord"

Elder Gerrit W. Gong

In the school of mortal life, the Lord invites us to learn and grow in lifelong and eternal ways by loving Him first and by strengthening one another in His love.

Strengthening one another in the Lord and in His love is embodied in the first and second great commandments. As the First Presidency letter recently taught, "The Savior's ministry exemplifies the two great commandments: 'Thou shalt love the Lord thy God with all thy heart, and with all thy soul, and with all thy mind' and 'Thou shalt love thy neighbour as thyself' (Matthew 22:37, 39). In that spirit, Jesus also taught, 'Ye are they whom I have chosen to minister unto this people' (3 Nephi 13:25)."[1] The song of our risen Savior's redeeming love celebrates the harmony of covenants (that connect us to God and to each other) and the Atonement of Jesus Christ (that helps us put off the natural man and woman and yield to the sanctifying enticing of the Holy Spirit [see Mosiah 3:19]).

That harmony is expressed in the plan of happiness, where we learn and grow by daily exercise of individual moral agency. Nor are we left to wander on our own, but are given a covenant path and the gift of the Holy Ghost. Alpha and Omega (see Doctrine and Covenants 61:1), the Lord Jesus Christ, is with us from the beginning. And He is with us to the end, when "God shall wipe away all tears from [our] eyes" (Revelation 7:17), except our tears of joy.

Our covenants connect us to God and to each other. Meant to be eternal, our covenants include God our Eternal Father and His Son, Jesus Christ. Eternal covenants can bring the power of God's love—to give hope and increase love; to lift and transform; to edify and sanctify; to redeem and exalt.

In the revelation of our true, divine selves through our covenants with God, we learn to recognize and love our brothers and sisters as He does. This deepening love and knowledge invites, empowers, and sanctifies us to know and, in our own way, to become more like Him.

The harmony of our covenants and the Atonement of Jesus Christ is heard in the melodies and descants as drawing on our Savior's Atonement helps us fulfill our covenants in a new and holier way. Together, our covenants and our Savior's Atonement can shape what we desire, perceive, and experience in daily mortality and prepare us for the sociality of heaven (see Doctrine and Covenants 130:2).

Through the Atonement of Jesus Christ, we find faith, strength, and trust to come unto Christ, knowing perfection is in Him. Such offers an escape from the otherwise always anxious treadmill of perfectionism. There may be some truth in the children's song "Let It Go"[2]—if "let it go" means "let go" of self-imposed worldly expectations that can never satisfy and if it also means "hold on" to the God-given heavenly hopes and promises the Lord offers.

Have you noticed that each ordinance calls us by our name and connects us by our name to the name of Jesus Christ?

Ordinances are universal and particular (or individual) at the same time. Years ago, as the high councilor responsible for stake baptisms, I noticed stake baptisms were outwardly the same but individually distinct. The baptismal ordinance was outwardly the same for each person but individually distinct in that each person baptized was called, one by one, by their name, and their name was connected by covenant to the name of the Father, and of the Son, and of the Holy Ghost.

Amazing grace is as universal and unique as our Savior Himself. A Lamb without blemish, He set the pattern by being baptized to fulfill all righteousness (see 2 Nephi 31:6). The scriptures call it, and our missionaries teach it as, the doctrine of Christ (see 2 Nephi 31:21; 3 Nephi 11:38–40). The doctrine of Christ includes "to follow the example of Jesus Christ by being baptized by someone holding the priesthood authority of God."[3] We enter through the gate of repentance and baptism by water, "and then cometh a remission of [our] sins by fire and by the Holy Ghost." The strait and narrow path—the covenant path— leads to eternal life (2 Nephi 31:17–18). It is part of how we are each strengthened in His love.

Our covenants and the Atonement of Jesus Christ connect in other ways as well.

We belong to each other. By divine covenant, we belong to God and to each other. Covenant belonging is a miracle. It is not possessive. It "suffereth long, and is kind." It "envieth not, . . . vaunteth not itself, is not puffed up" (1 Corinthians 13:4; see also Moroni 7:45). Covenant belonging gives roots and wings. It liberates through commitment. It enlarges through love.

In covenant belonging, we strengthen each other in His love, thereby coming more to love God and each other. This is in part because covenant belonging "seeketh not her own, is not easily provoked, thinketh no evil" (1 Corinthians 13:5). Covenant belonging "rejoiceth not in iniquity, but rejoiceth in the truth" (1 Corinthians 13:6). Covenant belonging is to come and see face to face, knowing even as we are known (see 1 Corinthians 13:12). Our covenant faithfulness is steadfast and immovable (see Mosiah 5:15; Alma 1:25).

Covenant belonging is to hope all things, to endure many things, and hope to be able to endure all things (see Articles of Faith 1:13; see also 1 Corinthians 13:7; Moroni 7:45). Covenant belonging is to keep the faith. It is not to give up on ourselves, on each other, or on God.

Covenant belonging is to delight with those who delight and to rejoice with those who have cause to rejoice and to stand as witnesses of God's tender mercies and daily miracles at all times and in all things and in all places (see Mosiah 18:8–9).

To belong to God and to each other in covenant belonging is to smile in unexpected places as we see with eyes to see and hear with ears to hear. He changes us and our relationships to become more like Him and His.

As we strengthen each other in His love, we are active participants in Leo Tolstoy's heroism of everyday living.

In one marriage relations class, a married student finally raised her hand and said to the teacher, "Pardon me, you keep saying marriage is hard. It is not marriage that is hard; life is hard, and marriage, with its ups and downs, can be a blessing where we get to face the joys and challenges of life together."

While eternal marriage is our ideal, infidelities, abuse of any kind, unsurmountable incompatibilities may necessitate immediate, protective action, also separation and possibly divorce. We know covenants are binding and eternal only by mutual consent of the parties affected and when confirmed by a merciful heaven's manifestation of the Holy Ghost, which the scriptures describe as the Holy Spirit of Promise. There is comfort, peace, and hope in the Lord's assurance that worthy individuals will receive all promised blessings.[4] It is part of His promise to strengthen each of us in His love, in His way, and in His time (see Doctrine and Covenants 88:68).

When I was a young bishop, an experience in our ward taught us about covenant belonging as manifested in the strengthening of one another in His love.

Our ward included many extraordinary families and individuals. Among them were the Hans and Fay Ritter family and the Larry and Tina O'Connor family. The Ritters and O'Connors, along with many others, were constantly ministering to others and were beloved by all.

One day our stake president gently asked if I would check on the Ritters. When I came to the Ritter home, they invited me in and we had a good visit. I noticed some sagging in the floor and a well-used kettle. Brother Ritter said, "Bishop, it's like this. Our water heater leaked, and warm water seeped through the floor. Termites came. That's why the floor sags a little. We had to shut off the water heater, and that's why we heat water in a kettle."

I asked Brother and Sister Ritter if I could discuss their situation with our ward council. There were initially reluctant, but finally agreed. Always other-oriented, on this occasion, a gift they gave was allowing others to join in serving together. Our ward council was amazing—everyone knew someone who could help with floors, walls, carpets, appliances, paint. Many came and helped in countless generous ways. Among them was Larry

O'Connor, a skilled builder who, with many generous others, was frequently at the Ritters' house.

Recently, Tina O'Connor, Larry's wife, recalled, "Larry and Jack Schwab and other quorum members would sometimes go to the Ritters' on Friday and stay all night." Tina said, "One Saturday morning I took them breakfast and there was Larry coming out of a bathroom holding plumbing tools. He and Jack were happy to be working together, though they clearly looked like they had been at it all night."

Tina added, "It was from men like Hans Ritter and Larry Chandler that my husband learned to become a man—kind, thoughtful, tender. As my Larry served together with such good men, including in the nursery," Tina said, "he became an even more wonderful husband and father."

When the house was finished, we all rejoiced.

Hans and Fay Ritter have been gone for some time, but I spoke recently with two of their sons, Ben and Stephen, who live with their families in Utah and Virginia.

Ben and Stephen remember that the quiet service of others maintained the dignity of their father, who worked tirelessly, they said, "sometimes two and three shifts at work," to take care of their family. Ben and Stephen said, "There was a wonderful feeling. We were working and serving together in love."

Stephen and Hans were Susan's and my home teachers for a time. Stephen told me, "I have been telling my elders quorum I home taught someone called to the Quorum of the Twelve." He laughed, "When the phone rang and you said you were Brother Gong, I was sure you were one of my quorum members joking with me."

Not too long after the Ritters' home was completed, something unexpected happened. While at a ward activity, Larry and Tina O'Connor received emergency word their home was on fire. They rushed to their home immediately and everywhere saw broken windows (to vent smoke) and walls punctured by fire axes (to check for hidden flames). Tina said, "We were devastated."

But then the ward came. Larry and Tina remember, "Everyone helped. We were able to put things back together. The whole ward came together in love. We were there as a family."

And who were among the first to come and among the last to leave as the O'Connor home was being rebuilt? Yes, Brother Hans Ritter and his family. Ben and Stephen are modest but remember their family coming to help the O'Connors. "We were all there together," Ben and Stephen remember. "That's the way service works. We all take care of each other, sometimes by helping others and sometimes by allowing others to help us."

To me, there can be a wondrous, virtuous, and harmonious circle as we strengthen each other in His love. The O'Connors help the Ritters, the Ritters help the O'Connors, and all the while a community of Latter-day Saints is being established. Each day, in myriad ways, we each need and can offer ministering love and support in small, simple, powerful, life-changing ways.

And thus we experience a double loaves and fishes miracle: first, a community of Saints can rally in magnificent selfless unity to address a dramatic need; and second, simultaneously, a fellowship of Saints can be knit together in love, through daily, loving ministering in many quiet circumstances (as in a family, a ward, a branch, or a community over many years), independent of any dramatic need.

All of this brings us back to where we began—the first and second great commandments and the invitation to be strengthened and to strengthen each other in the Lord's love. President Russell M. Nelson powerfully invites, "Our message to the world is simple and sincere: We invite all of God's children on both sides of the veil to come unto their Savior, receive the blessings of the holy temple, have enduring joy, and qualify for eternal life."[5] As we feast upon the words of Christ (see 2 Nephi 32:3) and put God first (see Matthew 6:33), the Lord strengthens and blesses every aspect of our lives. There is divine harmony and resonance in covenant belonging as we are strengthened in His love and as we strengthen each other in the Lord.

The words of the Apostle Paul echo the harmony of our covenants and the Atonement of the Lord Jesus Christ:

"Who shall separate us from the love of Christ? shall tribulation, or distress, or persecution, or famine, or nakedness, or peril, or sword? . . . For I am persuaded, that neither death, nor life, nor angels, nor principalities, nor powers, nor things present, nor things to come, nor height, nor depth, nor any other creature, shall be able to separate us from the love of God, which is in Christ Jesus our Lord" (Romans 8:35, 38–39).

Such is also my solemn testimony. I testify of God our Eternal Heavenly Father and His Son, Jesus Christ. They know us better and love us more than we know or love ourselves. This is why we can trust in the Lord with all our heart, and need not lean unto our own understanding (see Proverbs 3:5).

In 159 Houses of the Lord in forty-three countries, we can be strengthened in the Lord through our covenants and the Atonement of Jesus Christ. We are blessed by priesthood authority and continuing prophetic revelation from the Prophet Joseph Smith to our dear President Russell M. Nelson today. Events of recent days have made me even more certain of, and even more humbled by, the reality of restored doctrine, keys, ordinances, and covenants in The Church of Jesus Christ of Latter-day Saints as the "Lord's kingdom once again established on the earth, preparatory to the second coming of the Messiah" (Book of Mormon, Introduction).

The Book of Mormon: Another Testament of Jesus Christ and all the holy scriptures are the word of God.

Dear sisters, as you return to your places of abode, whether near or far, may you do so with a certainty the Lord loves you, each of you, *uno por uno*, one by one. He knows your goodness, your righteous hopes and desires, your immense talents and consecration, your concerns and joys.

Where there is illness or concern, in the office of my calling and in all humility, I bless you with peace and assurance, health and strength, the necessities of this life, according to the will of the Lord.

I bless you that the spiritual truths you have felt these past days will deepen your conversion and increase your faith and trust in our Heavenly Father and our Savior Jesus Christ and His Atonement.

May you know, by the power of the Holy Ghost, the truth of the continuing fruits and blessings of the Restoration, including as evidenced in the Prophet Joseph Smith, in the Book of Mormon, and our dear President Russell M. Nelson.

That we may each come to know our Savior better and become even more like Him, as we are strengthened in the Lord, and as we strengthen each other in the Lord and His love, I humbly pray.

Notes

The Watchman on the Tower: Listen to a Prophet's Voice
Kathy S. Andersen

1. Neil L. Andersen, "A Prophet of God," *Ensign,* May 2018, 25.
2. Neil L. Andersen, "A Prophet of God," 25.
3. Russell M. Nelson, "Revelation for the Church, Revelation for Our Lives," *Ensign,* May 2018, 96.
4. Russell M. Nelson, "Revelation for the Church, Revelation for Our Lives," 96.
5. Russell M. Nelson, "Revelation for the Church, Revelation for Our Lives," 96.
6. Russell M. Nelson, "Revelation for the Church, Revelation for Our Lives," 95.
7. Russell M. Nelson, "Revelation for the Church, Revelation for Our Lives," 96.
8. Russell M. Nelson, "Revelation for the Church, Revelation for Our Lives," 95.
9. Russell M. Nelson, "Revelation for the Church, Revelation for Our Lives," 95; paragraphing altered.
10. Russell M. Nelson, "Revelation for the Church, Revelation for Our Lives," 95; paragraphing altered.
11. Russell M. Nelson, "Revelation for the Church, Revelation for Our Lives," 95; paragraphing altered.
12. Russell M. Nelson, "Revelation for the Church, Revelation for Our Lives," 95; paragraphing altered.
13. See Thomas Kelly, "As the Dews from Heaven Distilling," *Hymns of The Church of Jesus Christ of Latter-day Saints* (Salt Lake City: The Church of Jesus Christ of Latter-day Saints, 1985), no. 149.
14. Russell M. Nelson, "Revelation for the Church, Revelation for Our Lives," 95, quoting Joseph Smith, in *Teachings of Presidents of the Church: Joseph Smith* (Salt Lake City: The Church of Jesus Christ of Latter-day Saints, 2007), 132.
15. Dallin H. Oaks, "Small and Simple Things," *Ensign,* May 2018, 91.
16. See Judith Mehr, *Moses and the Brass Serpent,* available at https://www.lds.org/media-library/images/moses-brass-serpent-39479; accessed 17 August 2018.

17. Harold B. Lee, in Conference Report, April 1946, 68.

18. Spencer W. Kimball, "In the World but Not of It," BYU devotional, 14 May 1968, quoted in *Brigham Young University Speeches of the Year* (Provo, UT: BYU Press, 1968), 3.

19. Ezra Taft Benson, "'Come unto Christ, and Be Perfected in Him,'" *Ensign,* May 1988, 84.

20. Russell M. Nelson, "Let Us All Press On," *Ensign,* May 2018, 118.

21. Russell M. Nelson, "Let Us All Press On," 118.

22. William Fowler, "We Thank Thee, O God, for a Prophet," *Hymns,* no. 19

A New and Holier Way of Ministering:
Strengthen One Another in the Lord
Kevin J Worthen

1. Jeffrey R. Holland, "'Be With and Strengthen Them,'" *Ensign*, May 2018, 101.

2. Henry B. Eyring, "Inspired Ministering," *Ensign,* May 2018, 62.

3. Gordon B. Hinckley, "Missionary Service," *First Worldwide Leadership Training Meeting,* 11 January 2003 (Salt Lake City: The Church of Jesus Christ of Latter-day Saints, 2003), 19; quoted in Richard G. Scott, "The Power of *Preach My Gospel,*" *Ensign,* May 2005, 29.

4. Richard G. Scott, "The Power of *Preach My Gospel,*" 29. See, for example, chapter 4, "How Do I Recognize and Understand the Spirit?" in *Preach My Gospel: A Guide to Missionary Service* (Salt Lake City: The Church of Jesus Christ of Latter-day Saints, 2004), 89–102.

5. See *Teaching the Gospel in the Savior's Way: A Guide to "Come, Follow Me: Learning Resources for Youth"* (Salt Lake City: The Church of Jesus Christ of Latter-day Saints, 2012).

6. See letter from the First Presidency of The Church of Jesus Christ of Latter-day Saints, 25 August 2017 (making the change effective on January 1, 2018); available at https://www.lds.org/bc/content/ldsorg/church/news/2017/10/05/15038_000.pdf; accessed 22 August 2018.

7. Russell M. Nelson, "Revelation for the Church, Revelation for Our Lives," *Ensign,* May 2018, 95, 96.

8. "The Border Guard," Mid-Island StoryTellers, available at http://midisland storytellers.com/uploads/3/2/4/1/3241687/the_border_guard.pdf; accessed 17 August 2018.

9. Russell M. Nelson, "Let Us All Press On," *Ensign,* May 2018, 118–19.

10. See Russell M. Nelson, "Revelation for the Church," 93–96.

11. Russell M. Nelson, "The Sabbath Is a Delight," *Ensign*, May 2015, 132.

12. See "Letter from the First Presidency of The Church of Jesus Christ of Latter-day Saints, 2 April 2018"; available at https://www.lds.org/ministering/first-presidency-letter; accessed 22 August 2018.

13. Henry B. Eyring, "Inspired Ministering," *Ensign*, May 2018, 62; emphasis added.

14. Henry B. Eyring, "His Spirit to Be with You," *Ensign*, May 2018, 88; emphasis added.

15. Henry B. Eyring, "Inspired Ministering," 64. In the same vein, Elder David A.

Bednar once observed, "Praying for others with all of the energy of our souls increases our capacity to hear and to heed the voice of the Lord" ("Pray Always," *Ensign*, November 2008, 43).

16. Jean B. Bingham, "Ministering as the Savior Does," *Ensign*, May 2018, 104–5.

17. See, for example, in the May 2018 *Ensign*, Dallin H. Oaks, "The Powers of the Priesthood," 65–68; Henry B. Eyring, "Inspired Ministering," 61–64; Jeffrey R. Holland, "Be With and Strengthen Them," 101–3; Gérald Caussé, "It Is All About People," 111–13; Bonnie L. Oscarson, "Young Women in the Work," 36–38; and Reyna I. Aburto, "With One Accord," 78–80—all of which contain stories of ministering experiences.

18. M. Russell Ballard, in *Invitation to Act* (video), 00:49–01:01, available at https://www.lds.org/media-library/video/2018-04-0070-invitation-to-act; accessed 17 August 2018.

19. Russell M. Nelson, "Ministering with the Power and Authority of God," *Ensign,* May 2018, 68; emphasis added.

20. While the document "The Living Christ" testifies that the resurrected Christ "visited among those He had loved in life," it also says that He "ministered among His 'other sheep' (John 10:16) in ancient America" ("The Living Christ: The Testimony of the Apostles," *Ensign*, April 2000, 2).

21. M. Russell Ballard, in "Invitation to Act," 00:15–00:42.

22. Harold B. Lee, "Be Loyal to the Royal within You," BYU devotional address, 11 September 1973; available at https://speeches.byu.edu/talks/harold-b-lee_loyal-royal-within/; accessed 17 August 2018.

23. "The Family: A Proclamation to the World," *Ensign*, November 2010, 129.

24. Russell M. Nelson, "Ministering with the Power and Authority of God," 68.

25. Jean B. Bingham, "Ministering as the Savior Does," 104.

Christlike Connections
Bonnie H. Cordon

1. Kathy Kipp Clayton, "You Are Royalty," *Ensign*, August 2016, 23.

2. See Joseph Stein, "Fiddler on the Roof," in *Great Musicals of the American Theatre*, vol. 1, ed. Stanley Richards (Radnor, PA: Chilton Book Company, 1973), 393.

3. Gordon B. Hinckley, *Discourses of President Gordon B. Hinckley: Volume 1: 1995–1999* (Salt Lake City: Deseret Book, 2005), 544–45.

4. See Joy D. Jones, "Value beyond Measure," *Ensign*, November 2017, 13–15.

5. Spencer W. Kimball, *Teachings of Presidents of the Church: Spencer W. Kimball* (Salt Lake City: The Church of Jesus Christ of Latter-day Saints, 2006), 85.

6. Russell M. Nelson, "A Plea to My Sisters," *Ensign*, November 2015, 96.

"Love One Another, as I Have Loved You"
Jennifer Brinkerhoff Platt

1. See Dallin H. Oaks, "Introductory Message" (address given at the seminar for new mission presidents, 25 June 2017), 2; as quoted by Elder D. Todd

Christofferson, "The Living Bread Which Came Down from Heaven," *Ensign*, November 2017, 37.

2. After Christ miraculously fed the 5,000, the multitudes followed Him seeking continual nourishment. The Savior then teaches of His ministry and capacity as the only source of everlasting life. Rather than temporal sustenance, He offers the bread of life . . . Himself. If we choose to partake and follow the Savior, we can live forever with Him. See John 6:25–58.

3. See Lisa Ann Jackson, "Church Sends Aid to Ethiopia," *Ensign*, June 2003, 76–77, and Sarah Jane Weaver, "Fast for Ethiopia accelerated work," *Church News*, 6 February 2010, and Glenn L. Pace's book *Safe Journey: An African Adventure* (Salt Lake City: Deseret Book, 2003).

4. Jennifer A. Brinkerhoff, "Being a Good Ethiopian Woman: Participation in the 'Buna' (Coffee) Ceremony and Identity," doctoral dissertation, Arizona State University, 2011; available at https://repository.asu.edu/attachments/56829/content/Brinkerhoff_asu_0010E_10790.pdf; accessed 17 August 2018.

5. Brinkerhoff, "Being a Good Ethiopian Woman," 145; punctuation and grammar standardized.

6. For more on ritualizing your life, see Jennifer Brinkerhoff Platt, *Living Your Covenants Every Day* (Salt Lake City: Deseret Book, 2013).

7. See LDS Bible Dictionary, s.v. "prayer," 752–53.

8. Personal correspondence in the author's possession.

9. Russell M. Nelson, "Divine Love," *Ensign*, February 2003, 20.

10. For more on distinguishing between doctrines, principles, and application, see Elder David A. Bednar's book *Act in Doctrine* (Salt Lake City: Deseret Book, 2012).

11. See *Come, Follow Me: Learning Resources for Youth* (website); available at https://lds.org/youth; accessed 24 October 2018; see also *Basic Doctrines* (2012); available at https://lds.org/manual/basic-doctrines; accessed 24 October 2018.

12. Elder Richard G. Scott spoke on several occasions about distinguishing principles. See, for instance, "Acquiring Spiritual Knowledge," *Ensign*, November 1993, 86–88.

13. This statement, or one similar—others use similar promises, such as, "shall be led towards the promised land," or "shall prosper in the land of promise," for example—is used throughout the Book of Mormon; see 1 Nephi 2:20, 22; 4:14; 17:13; 2 Nephi 1:20; 4:4; Jarom 1:9; Omni 1:6 (an example of a negative if-then statement); and Alma 9:13; 50:20.

14. See Susan Evans McCloud, "Lord, I Would Follow Thee," *Hymns of The Church of Jesus Christ of Latter-day Saints* (Salt Lake City: The Church of Jesus Christ of Latter-day Saints, 1985), no. 220.

15. Boyd K. Packer, "Little Children," *Ensign*, November 1986, 17; paragraphing altered.

16. See Naomi W. Randall, "I Am a Child of God," *Hymns*, no. 301.

17. Russell M. Nelson, "Ministering with the Power and Authority of God," *Ensign*, May 2018, 75.

18. Russell M. Nelson, "A Plea to My Sisters," *Ensign*, November 2015, 97.

19. Cori Connors, "The Knife," *Guideposts*, March 1997, 36.

20. Sabine Baring-Gould, "Onward Christian Soldiers," *Hymns*, no. 246.

"A Plea to My Sisters": To Fill the Measure of Our Creation
Jennifer Reeder

1. See Gordon B. Hinckley, "Women of the Church," *Ensign*, November 1996, 67–70 and Russell M. Nelson, "A Plea to My Sisters," *Ensign*, November 2015, 95–98.

2. "A Message from the First Presidency," 16 January 2018; available at https://www.lds.org/bc/content/ldsorg/church/news/2018/01/19/2018-01-1000-a-message-from-the-first-presidency.pdf; accessed 20 August 2018.

3. Russell M. Nelson, Facebook post, 17 January 2018, available at https://www.facebook.com/lds.russell.m.nelson/posts/1604867749580655; accessed 20 August 2018.

4. Russell M. Nelson, "A Plea to My Sisters," 97.

5. See Sheri Dew, "Knowing Who You Are—And Who You Have Always Been," BYU Women's Conference, 4 May 2001; in *At the Pulpit: 185 Years of Discourses by Latter-day Saint Women,* Jennifer Reeder and Kate Holbrook, eds. (Salt Lake City: Church Historian's Press, 2017), 263–75.

6. Bonnie D. Parkin, "Personal Ministry: Sacred and Precious," BYU devotional, 13 February 2007; available at https://speeches.byu.edu/wp-content/uploads/pdf/Parkin_Bonnie_2007_02.pdf; accessed 20 August 2018.

7. See Noah Webster, *American Dictionary of the English Language*, 1828 facsimile edition (Chesapeake, VA: Foundation for American Christian Education, 1967), s.v. "fill" and "measure"; see also *Oxford English Dictionary* (Oxford: Oxford University Press, 1998), s.v. "fill" and "measure."

8. Patricia T. Holland, "Filling the Measure of Your Creation," BYU devotional, 17 January 1989; available at https://speeches.byu.edu/wp-content/uploads/pdf/Holland_Patricia_1989_01.pdf; accessed 20 August 2018.

9. Noah Webster, *American Dictionary of the English Language*, s.v. "expound" and "exhort."

10. "Nauvoo Relief Society Minute Book," 7–8, The Joseph Smith Papers; available at http://www.josephsmithpapers.org/paper-summary/nauvoo-relief-society-minute-book/4; accessed 20 August 2018; see also *The First Fifty Years of Relief Society: Key Documents in the History of Latter-day Saint Women*, Jill Mulvay Derr, Carol Cornwall Madsen, Kate Holbrook, and Matthew J. Grow, eds. (Salt Lake City: Church Historian's Press, 2016), 32.

11. Joseph Smith told the women of the Nauvoo Relief Society on 28 April 1842, "I now turn the key to you in the name of God and this Society shall rejoice and knowledge and intelligence shall flow down from this time—this is the beginning of better days, to this Society." ("Nauvoo Relief Society Minute Book," [40], The Joseph Smith Papers; available at http://www.josephsmithpapers.org/paper-summary/nauvoo-relief-society-minute-book/37; accessed 20 August, 2018; see also *First Fifty Years of Relief Society*, Derr et al., eds., 59).

12. See Dallin H. Oaks, "The Keys and Authority of the Priesthood," *Ensign*, May 2014, 49–52.

13. See Russell M. Nelson, "A Plea to My Sisters."

14. Spencer W. Kimball, "The Role of Righteous Women," *Ensign*, November 1979, 102.

15. Boyd K. Packer, "The Relief Society," *Ensign*, November 1978, 8.

16. See Russell M. Nelson, "A Plea to My Sisters," 96.

17. Eliza R. Snow, "Sketch of My Life," in *The Personal Writings of Eliza Roxcy Snow*, Maureen Ursenbach Beecher, ed. (Logan, UT: Utah State University Press, 2000), 35.

18. Russell M. Nelson, "A Plea to My Sisters," 97.

19. Lehi Ward, Utah Stake, Relief Society Minutes and Records, vol. 1, 1868–1879, 27 October 1869, 30, Church History Library; in *At the Pulpit: 185 Years of Discourses of Latter-day Saint Women*, Jennifer Reeder and Kate Holbrook, eds. (Salt Lake City: Church Historian's Press, 2017), 48.

20. *Deseret Evening News,* 8 October 1879, 2; see also Jennifer Reeder, "'Power for the Accomplishment of Greater Good': Zina Diantha Huntington Young (1821–1901)," in *Women of Faith in the Latter Days: Volume Two, 1821–1845*, Richard E. Turley Jr. and Brittany A. Chapman, eds. (Salt Lake City: Deseret Book, 2012), 446.

21. [Emmeline B. Wells], "A Distinguished Woman," *Woman's Exponent* 10, no. 15 (1 January 1882): 115.

22. "First General Conference of the Relief Society," *Woman's Exponent* 17, no. 22 (15 April 1889): 172–73.

23. [Emmeline B. Wells], "A Representative Woman," *Woman's Exponent* 11, no. 8 (15 September 1882): 59.

24. Susa Young Gates, *History of the Young Ladies' Mutual Improvement Association* (Salt Lake City: Deseret News, 1911), 29–31.

25. Emmeline B. Wells, "The Jubilee Celebration," *Woman's Exponent* 20, no. 17 (15 March 1892): 132.

26. Emmeline B. Wells, "Sisters Be in Earnest," *Woman's Exponent* 5, no. 10 (October 15, 1876): 76.

27. Emmeline B. Wells, "The Mission of Saving Grain," Relief Society Magazine 2, no. 2 (February 1915): 49.

28. Committees on the Grain Movement, Minutes, 17 November 1876, in "General Meeting of Central and Ward Committees, on the Grain Movement," *Woman's Exponent* 5, no. 13 (1 December 1876): 99; in *First Fifty Years of Relief Society*, Derr et al., eds., 399–404.

29. Russell M. Nelson, "A Plea to My Sisters," 97.

30. Russell M. Nelson, "A Plea to My Sisters," 97.

31. Louisa Barnes Pratt, Journal and Autobiography, in *The History of Louisa Barnes Pratt: Mormon Missionary Widow and Pioneer,* S. George Ellsworth, ed. (Logan, UT: Utah State University Press, 1998), 65–66, 78, 81–82, 86–90.

32. Pratt, A, Part 1, 26 July 1850 to January 1851, 27 August 1851; in Ellsworth, *The History of Louisa Barnes Pratt,* 141; punctuation modernized.

33. Caroline Barnes Crosby, journal, 15 September 1851; in *No Place to Call Home: The 1807–1857 Life Writings of Caroline Barnes Crosby, Chronicler of Outlying Mormon Communities,* Edward Leo Lyman, Susan Ward Payne, and S. George Ellsworth, eds. (Logan, UT: Utah State University Press, 2005), 134.

34. Pratt, Memoirs, 15 September 1851 to 1 February 1852, 12 November 1851; in Ellsworth, *The History of Louisa Barnes Pratt,* 150.

35. Russell M. Nelson, "A Plea to My Sisters," 96–97.

36. *The Journals of Addison Pratt*, S. George Ellsworth, ed. (Salt Lake City: University of Utah Press, 1990), 513.

37. Russell M. Nelson, "A Plea to My Sisters," 97.

38. Nauvoo Relief Society, 31 March 1842, 17–18; in *The First Fifty Years of Relief Society*, Derr et al., eds., 40.

39. Marjorie Pay Hinckley, in *Glimpses into the Life and Heart of Marjorie Pay Hinckley*, Virginia H. Pearce, ed. (Salt Lake City: Deseret Book, 1999), 254–55.

40. Julia Mavimbela, "I Speak from My Heart: The Story of a Black South African Woman," in *Women of Wisdom and Knowledge: Talks Selected from BYU Women's Conference*, Marie Cornwall and Susan Howe, eds. (Salt Lake City: Deseret Book, 1990), 68.

41. Carol Cornwall Madsen, in introduction to Mavimbela, "I Speak from My Heart," 63.

42. Nauvoo Relief Society, 28 April 1842, 38; in *The First Fifty Years of Relief Society,* Derr et al., eds., 58.

43. Mavimbela, "I Speak from My Heart," 63.

44. Russell M. Nelson, "A Plea to My Sisters," 96.

45. Nauvoo Relief Society Minutes, 37; in *The First Fifty Years of Relief Society,* Derr et al., eds., 57; spelling standardized.

46. Carol R. Gray, "Can I Have a Hug, Please?" manuscript, Church History Library; see also R. Scott Lloyd, "Pioneers in Every Land Lecture Features Story of British Housewife Humanitarian," *Church News*, 28 October 2015; available at https://www.lds.org/church/news/pioneers-in-every-land-lecture-features-story-of-british-housewife-humanitarian; accessed 21 August 2018.

47. Boyd K. Packer, "Relief Society," *Ensign*, November 1978, 8.

48. Gray, "Can I Have a Hug, Please?"

49. Russell M. Nelson, "A Plea to My Sisters," 97.

50. Gray, "Can I Have a Hug, Please?"

51. Russell M. Nelson, "A Plea to My Sisters," 97.

Choosing Personal Responsibility and Accountability
Lauren A. Barnes

1. Delbert L. Stapley, "Using Our Free Agency," *Ensign*, May 1975, 21.

2. Lynn G. Robbins, "Be 100 Percent Responsible," BYU devotional, 22 August 2017, 1; available at https://speeches.byu.edu/wp-content/uploads/pdf/Robbins_Lynn_2017-08-22.pdf; accessed 21 August 2018.

3. *Merriam-Webster's Collegiate Dictionary, Eleventh Edition* (Springfield, MA: Merriam-Webster, 2003), s.v. "accountability."

4. Lynn G. Robbins, "Be 100 Percent Responsible," 1; see also Doctrine and Covenants 101:78.

5. D. Todd Christofferson, "Moral Agency," *Ensign*, June 2009, 47, 48.

6. Dallin H. Oaks, "Weightier Matters," BYU devotional , 9 February 1999, 2; available at https://speeches.byu.edu/wp-content/uploads/pdf/Oaks_Dallin_1999_02.pdf; accessed 21 August 2018.

7. *LDS Topical Guide* , s.v. "responsibility"; available at https://www.lds.org /scriptures/tg/responsibility; accessed 21 August 2018.

8. Lynn G. Robbins, "Be 100 Percent Responsible," 2.

9. Lynn G. Robbins, "Be 100 Percent Responsible," 2.

10. Lynn G. Robbins, "Be 100 Percent Responsible," 2–3.

11. Lynn G. Robbins, "Be 100 Percent Responsible," 4.

12. Lynn G. Robbins, "Be 100 Percent Responsible," 4.

13. Viktor E. Frankl, *Man's Search for Meaning* (Boston: Beacon Press, 2006), 66.

14. *Merriam-Webster's Collegiate Dictionary, Eleventh Edition*, s.v. "personal."

15. Gordon B. Hinckley, "Stay on the High Road," *Ensign*, May 2004, 113.

16. "The Family: A Proclamation to the World," *Ensign*, November 2010, 129.

17. For an excellent explanation of *ezer kenegdo* (translated in the KJV as "help-meet"), see Bruce K. Satterfield, "The Family under Siege: The Role of Man and Woman," Ricks College Education Week presentation, 7 June 2001, 6; available at http://emp.byui.edu/SATTERFIELDB/PDF/Role%20of% 20Man%20and%20Woman.pdf; accessed 21 August 2018.

18. Lynn G. Robbins, "Be 100 Percent Responsible," 7.

Up, Awake, Ye Defenders of Zion
Joy D. Jones

1. M. Russell Ballard, "Standing for Truth and Right," *Ensign*, November 1997, 37.

2. Personal correspondence in the author's possession.

3. Joseph Smith, in *Autobiography of Parley P. Pratt*, Parley P. Pratt Jr., ed. (Salt Lake City: Deseret Book, 1938), 180.

4. Martin Luther, in Roland H. Bainton, *Here I Stand: A Life of Martin Luther* (Peabody, MA: Hendrickson Publishers, 2009), 180.

5. Robert D. Hales, "'Come, Follow Me' by Practicing Christian Love and Service," *Ensign*, November 2016, 24.

6. Heather C., "Staying Strong in the Classroom," *New Era*, January 2012, 42.

7. Bonnie L. Oscarson, "Defenders of the Family Proclamation," *Ensign,* May 2015, 17.

8. Jeffrey R. Holland, "The Cost—and Blessings—of Discipleship," *Ensign*, May 2014, 6.

9. *Daughters in My Kingdom: The History and Work of Relief Society* (Salt Lake City: The Church of Jesus Christ of Latter-day Saints, 2011), 57.

10. Sharon Eubank, "Turn On your Light," *Ensign,* November 2017, 7.

"That We May All Sit Down in Heaven Together"
Sharon Eubank and Reyna I. Aburto

1. Relief Society Minutes, Mar. 24, 1842, "Nauvoo Relief Society Minute Book," pp. 18–19, The Joseph Smith Papers; available at http://www .josephsmithpapers.org/paper-summary/nauvoo-relief-society-minute-book/16; accessed 22 August 2018.

2. Russell M. Nelson, April 2018 General Authority training, transcript in authors' possession.

3. Kylee Beckstrom, Facebook comment, 2 April 2018; available at https://www.facebook.com/RSGeneralPresident/photos/a.652039461630846/941671179334338/; accessed 22 August 2018.

4. Emily Felsted Brady, Facebook comment, 2 April 2018; available at https://www.facebook.com/RSGeneralPresident/photos/a.652039461630846/941671179334338/; accessed 22 August 2018.

5. Christina Pay, Facebook comment, 2 April 2018; available at https://www.facebook.com/RSGeneralPresident/photos/a.652039461630846/941671179334338/; accessed 22 August 2018.

6. See Jeffrey R. Holland, "'Be With and Strengthen Them,'" *Ensign*, May 2018, 102–3.

7. Russell M. Nelson, "Revelation for the Church, Revelation for Our Lives," *Ensign*, May 2018, 96.

8. Grant Emery, Facebook comment, 2 April 2018; available at https://www.facebook.com/RSGeneralPresident/photos/a.652039461630846/941671179334338/; accessed 22 August 2018.

9. Henry B. Eyring, "Walk with Me," *Ensign*, May 2017, 82.

10. Henry B. Eyring, "Walk with Me," *Ensign*, May 2017, 82.

11. Jean B. Bingham, "Ministering as the Savior Does," *Ensign*, May 2018, 106, quoting Russell T. Osguthorpe, "What If Love Were Our Only Motive?" BYU devotional, 8 March 2011, 7; available at https://speeches.byu.edu/wp-content/uploads/pdf/Osguthorpe_Russell_2011_03.pdf; accessed 22 August 2018.

Value beyond Measure: Our Relationship with
an All-Knowing and Loving Heavenly Father
Mary Williams

1. Spencer W. Kimball, "Privileges and Responsibilities of Sisters," *Ensign*, November 1978, 105.

2. Joy D. Jones, "Value beyond Measure," *Ensign*, November 2017, 15.

3. Dieter F. Uchtdorf, "A Yearning for Home," *Ensign*, November 2017, 21.

4. See Naomi W. Randall, "I Am a Child of God," *Hymns of The Church of Jesus Christ of Latter-day Saints* (Salt Lake City: The Church of Jesus Christ of Latter-day Saints, 1985), no. 30.

5. "Young Women Theme"; available at https://www.lds.org/young-women/personal-progress/young-women-theme; accessed 21 August 2018.

6. "The Family: A Proclamation to the World," *Ensign*, November 2010, 129.

7. Boyd K. Packer, "To Young Women and Men," *Ensign,* May 1989, 54.

8. See Janice Kapp Perry, "A Child's Prayer," *Children's Songbook* (Salt Lake City: The Church of Jesus Christ of Latter-day Saints, 1989), 12.

9. Joy D. Jones, "Value beyond Measure," 13.

10. Dieter F. Uchtdorf, "A Yearning for Home," 21.

11. In Bryant S. Hinckley, *Sermons and Missionary Services of Melvin Joseph Ballard* (Salt Lake City: Deseret Book, 1949), 156.

12. Thomas S. Monson, "We Never Walk Alone," *Ensign*, November 2013, 123–24.

13. Russell M. Nelson, "The Book of Mormon: What Would Your Life Be Like without It?" *Ensign*, November 2017, 61.

14. Russell M. Nelson, "The Book of Mormon: What Would Your Life Be Like without It?" 62–63.

15. Brigham Young, in *Journal of Discourses,* 26 vols. (Liverpool: Latter-day Saints' Book Depot, 1854–86), 8:339.

16. Henry B. Eyring, "O Remember, Remember," *Ensign*, November 2007, 67.

17. Brian K. Taylor, "Am I a Child of God?" *Ensign*, May 2018, 13.

18. W. Craig Zwick, "Lord, Wilt Thou Cause That My Eyes May Be Opened," *Ensign*, November 2017, 98.

19. Dale G. Renlund, "Through God's Eyes," *Ensign*, November 2015, 94.

Waiting Upon the Lord
Annalece Boothe Misiego

1. See Gordon B. Hinckley, "Put Your Shoulder to the Wheel," *New Era*, July 2000, 7.

2. Jeffrey R. Holland, "Tomorrow the Lord Will Do Wonders among You," *Ensign*, May 2016, 125–26.

3. See Richard G. Scott, "Temple Worship: The Source of Strength and Power in Times of Need," *Ensign*, May 2009, 43–45.

4. Jeffrey R. Holland, "Tomorrow the Lord Will Do Wonders among You," 126.

5. Jeffrey R. Holland, "Banishing All Shadows," BYU commencement, 26 April 2018; available at https://speeches.byu.edu/wp-content/uploads/pdf/Comm_2018_Apr_Holland.pdf; accessed 22 August 2018.

Our Savior's Love
Susan L. Gong

1. Russell M. Nelson, April 2018 General Authority training, transcript in author's possession.

2. See Bible Dictionary, s.v. "Burial," 627.

3. Brian Kershisnik, *She Will Find What Is Lost*, used with permission.

"Strengthen One Another in the Lord"
Elder Gerrit W. Gong

1. "Letter from the First Presidency of The Church of Jesus Christ of Latter-day Saints, 2 April 2018"; available at https://www.lds.org/ministering/first-presidency-letter; accessed 22 August 2018.

2. Kristen Anderson-Lopez and Robert Lopez, "Let It Go," *Frozen* (Anaheim, CA: Disney, 2013).

3. *Preach My Gospel* (Salt Lake City: The Church of Jesus Christ of Latter-day Saints, 2004), 66.

4. See *Handbook 2: Administering the Church* (Salt Lake City: The Church of Jesus Christ of Latter-day Saints, 2010), 1.3.3.

5. Russell M. Nelson, "Let Us All Press On," *Ensign*, May 2018, 118–19.

Contributors

Reyna I. Aburto was born in Nicaragua, and married Carlos Aburto of Mexico in the Jordan River Utah Temple in 1993. They are both converts to The Church of Jesus Christ of Latter-day Saints, and they have three children and two grandchildren. She studied industrial engineering for four years at Universidad Centroamerica, and earned an AAS degree in computer science from Utah Valley University. She owns a small translation business with her husband, having worked in the language industry for more than twenty-five years. Sister Aburto was called to be the second counselor in the Relief Society General Presidency in 2017, after having served on the Primary general board. She has also served extensively in the Relief Society, Sunday School, Young Women, Primary, and Scouting organizations in her ward and stake.

Elder Neil L. and Sister Kathy S. Andersen met as undergraduate students and both graduated from Brigham Young University. They were married on March 20, 1975, and are the parents of two sons and two daughters, and now enjoy seventeen wonderful grandchildren. They made their home in Tampa, Florida, until called with their young family to the France Bordeaux Mission in 1989. After Elder Andersen's call to the First Quorum of the Seventy in 1993, they were again sent to Europe, and later served for four years in Brazil. Elder Andersen was called to the Quorum of the Twelve Apostles on April 4, 2009. Sister Andersen has accompanied her husband on assignments throughout the world, as well as serving as a stake Young Women president, a regional public communications director, an early morning seminary teacher, and a Gospel Doctrine teacher.

Lauren A. Barnes is an assistant professor and the director of clinical training for the Marriage and Family Therapy program in the School of Family Life at Brigham Young University. She earned her bachelor's, master's, and PhD degrees from BYU. Prior to her faculty appointment at BYU in 2013, she worked as a therapist at Center for Change, treating girls and women struggling with eating disorders. She continues to maintain a small private practice. She currently serves as the stake primary president in her stake. She and her husband, Aaron, are the happy parents of two lively young children.

Bonnie H. Cordon was serving as the first counselor in the Primary General Presidency when she was called to be the Young Women General President in 2018. She was born in Idaho Falls, Idaho, and graduated with a bachelor's degree in education from Brigham Young University, where she met her husband, Derek. She worked in management in the software industry. She has served in the Church in the Primary, Young Women, and Relief Society auxiliaries at both the stake and ward level, and has taught early-morning seminary. She and her husband are the parents of four children.

Sharon Eubank was born in Redding, California. She served as a full-time missionary in the Finland Helsinki Mission and earned a bachelor's degree in English from Brigham Young University. She has worked as an ESL teacher in Japan, as a legislative aide in the US Senate, and owned a retail education store in Provo, Utah. At the time of her call as the first counselor in the Relief Society General Presidency, she was the director of LDS Charities, which employment she continues as she serves in the Relief Society. She has also served in numerous ward and stake Sunday School, Relief Society, Young Women, and Primary callings, as well as serving on the Relief Society general board from

2009 to 2012. She loves history, homemade pie, and crossword puzzles. She has a strong testimony of the happiness that comes from following Christ.

ELDER GERRIT W. GONG was sustained as a member of the Quorum of the Twelve Apostles in March 2018. He was born in Redwood City, California, in 1953. He earned a BA in Asian and university studies from Brigham Young University, then earned Master of Philosophy and Doctor of Philosophy degrees from Oxford University, where he was a Rhodes Scholar. He worked for the US State Department for many years, then as an assistant to the president for planning and assessment at BYU until 2010, when he was called as a General Authority Seventy. He served as a member of the Presidency of the Seventy from 2015 to his call to the Twelve. He has served in numerous Church callings, including as a full-time missionary in Taiwan, a high councilor, high priests group leader, stake Sunday School president, seminary teacher, bishop, stake mission president, stake president, and Area Seventy.

SUSAN L. GONG was raised in Taylorsville, Utah, earned a BA in English literature and an MA in creative writing from Brigham Young University, and served a full-time Mandarin-speaking mission in Taiwan. She taught advanced composition and first-year Chinese classes at BYU, Chinese classes at Provo High School, and worked as the co-coordinator for Chinese immersion programs in Utah elementary schools, and as the series editor for Step by Step, a series of basic Chinese illustrated readers for young Mandarin learners. Sister Gong met Elder Gong at the Provo Missionary Training Center when he was giving presentations about Chinese culture to missionaries going to Taiwan, of which she was one. They married in 1980 in the Salt Lake Temple, and are the parents of four sons.

JOY D. JONES is the thirteenth General President of the Primary. She was born in The Dalles, Oregon. She earned an associate of science degree at BYU, and has worked as a dispatcher for the US Forest Service, an administrative assistant, and a medical assistant. She and her husband, Robert, are the parents of five children and have twenty-one grandchildren. She enjoys playing with her grandchildren, temple and family history work, cooking and nutrition, and hiking and camping.

ANNALECE BOOTHE MISIEGO began performing at the age of three and has enjoyed the industry ever since. Originally from Spanish Fork, Utah, Annalece has danced and sung her way around the world, performing in mainland China, Korea, Hong Kong, Finland, Sweden, Norway, Denmark, and across the United States. She received her BA in theatre arts studies with a music dance theatre emphasis from Brigham Young University. Annalece has been teaching for thirteen years and has been a guest instructor at BYU, Utah Valley University, and Nanjing University in Nanjing, China. Annalece and her husband, Javier, are the parents of three lovely little girls.

JENNIFER BRINKERHOFF PLATT believes in making the most of life and living intentionally. She and her husband, Jed, along with their two children, find joy in the ordinary. She holds a PhD in lifespan developmental psychology from Arizona State University. She is a professor of religious education at Brigham Young University–Idaho, having previously taught at BYU–Provo and for the Church Educational System. Few things bring her more joy than teaching the gospel of Jesus Christ to others. She is passionate about helping individuals recognize their divine worth, identify and live their life mission, and own their greatness.

JENNIFER REEDER is the nineteenth-century women's history specialist at the Church History Department of The Church of Jesus Christ of Latter-day Saints. She holds a PhD in American history from George Mason University with an emphasis in women's history, religious history, memory, and material culture. Her master's degree is from New York University in history, archival management, and documentary editing. Her coedited publications include *At the Pulpit: 185 Years of Discourses by Latter-day Saint Women* (2017) and *The Witness of Women: Firsthand Experiences and Testimonies of the Restoration* (2016).

MARY WILLIAMS was born in Payson, Utah. She is an associate professor and former associate dean in the Brigham Young University College of

Nursing. She earned her BS in nursing from BYU, her MS in cardio-vascular nursing from the University of Utah, and her PhD in clinical research from the University of Arizona. Prior to coming to BYU, she worked at LDS Hospital in Salt Lake City as a staff nurse and head nurse. Following the death of her sister, she assumed responsibility for the care of four of her six children and now has the blessing of fifteen grandchildren. She has served in numerous Church callings, including stake Young Women president, ward Relief Society president, ward Young Women president, and full-time missionary. She serves on the BYU Women's Conference committee. She loves gardening, traveling, and spending time with her grandchildren. She has a strong testimony of the power of knowing your identity as a beloved child of Heavenly Father, who is aware of every detail of your life.

KEVIN J WORTHEN began serving as president of Brigham Young University in 2014. He was raised in Price, Utah, and is a BYU graduate in political science and law. He has served in the Church as a bishop and stake president and as an Area Seventy. He and his wife, Peggy, are the parents of three children and have five grandchildren.